The Middle East /

1. **Most items may be checked out for two weeks and renewed for the same period.** Additional restrictions may apply to high demand items.

2. A fine is charged for each school day material is not returned according to the above rule.

3. All damage to materials beyond reasonable wear and all losses shall be paid for by the borrower.

4. Each borrower is responsible for all items checked out on his/her library record and for all fines accruing on the same.

5. Library privileges may be restricted for borrowers who do not return overdue material fines in a timely fa

The Middle East

Other books in the Current Controversies series

The Middle East

Debra A. Miller, Book Editor

GREENHAVEN PRESS
A part of Gale, Cengage Learning

GALE
CENGAGE Learning™

Detroit • New York • San Francisco • New Haven, Conn • Waterville, Maine • London

Christine Nasso, *Publisher*
Elizabeth Des Chenes, *Managing Editor*

© 2008 Greenhaven Press, a part of Gale, Cengage Learning.

For more information, contact:
Greenhaven Press
27500 Drake Rd.
Farmington Hills, MI 48331-3535
Or you can visit our Internet site at gale.cengage.com

LIBRARY OF CONGRESS CATALOGING-IN-PUBLICATION DATA

The Middle East / Debra A. Miller, book editor.
p. cm. -- (Current controversies)
Includes bibliographical references and index.
ISBN-13: 978-0-7377-3960-2 (hardcover)
ISBN-13: 978-0-7377-3961-9 (pbk.)
1. Middle East--Relations--United States. 2. United States--Relation--Middle East.
3. War on Terrorism, 2001- 4. Iraq War, 2003- 5. Arab-Israeli conflict. I. Miller,
Debra A.
DS63.2.U5M473 2007
303.48'256073--dc22

2007037428

Printed in the United States of America
2 3 4 5 6 7 12 11 10 09 08

Contents

Chapter 1: Why Is the Middle East a Conflict Area?

The Iraq war has cost more than three thousand American lives, caused hundreds of thousands of Iraqi deaths and injuries, contributed to the largest budget deficit and national debt in American history, and ignited sectarianism, massive daily killings, and de facto civil war in Iraq.

No: The United States Should Not Withdraw Its Troops from Iraq

Although there are no easy solutions to the violence in Iraq, American troops are still necessary to protect civilians from violence, eradicate al Qaeda terrorists, and give Iraqi security forces and the Iraqi government time to develop.

Chapter 3: Can the Israeli-Palestinian Conflict Be Resolved?

A majority of Palestinians are willing to accept a peace agreement providing for recognition of Israel in exchange for a Palestinian state, but Israel and the United States must agree to peace negotiations without preconditions.

No: The Israeli-Palestinian Conflict Cannot Be Resolved

The chief rationale for maintaining a U.S. presence in the Middle East—the threat to oil supplies from the Soviet Union—has disappeared, and continued U.S. involvement in the region only ignites anti-Americanism and terrorism.

Foreword

By definition, controversies are "discussions of questions in which opposing opinions clash" (Webster's Twentieth Century Dictionary Unabridged). Few would deny that controversies are a pervasive part of the human condition and exist on virtually every level of human enterprise. Controversies transpire between individuals and among groups, within nations and between nations. Controversies supply the grist necessary for progress by providing challenges and challengers to the status quo. They also create atmospheres where strife and warfare can flourish. A world without controversies would be a peaceful world; but it also would be, by and large, static and prosaic.

The Series' Purpose

The purpose of the Current Controversies series is to explore many of the social, political, and economic controversies dominating the national and international scenes today. Titles selected for inclusion in the series are highly focused and specific. For example, from the larger category of criminal justice, Current Controversies deals with specific topics such as police brutality, gun control, white collar crime, and others. The debates in Current Controversies also are presented in a useful, timeless fashion. Articles and book excerpts included in each title are selected if they contribute valuable, long-range ideas to the overall debate. And wherever possible, current information is enhanced with historical documents and other relevant materials. Thus, while individual titles are current in focus, every effort is made to ensure that they will not become quickly outdated. Books in the Current Controversies series will remain important resources for librarians, teachers, and students for many years.

In addition to keeping the titles focused and specific, great care is taken in the editorial format of each book in the series. Book introductions and chapter prefaces are offered to provide background material for readers. Chapters are organized around several key questions that are answered with diverse opinions representing all points on the political spectrum. Materials in each chapter include opinions in which authors clearly disagree as well as alternative opinions in which authors may agree on a broader issue but disagree on the possible solutions. In this way, the content of each volume in Current Controversies mirrors the mosaic of opinions encountered in society. Readers will quickly realize that there are many viable answers to these complex issues. By questioning each author's conclusions, students and casual readers can begin to develop the critical thinking skills so important to evaluating opinionated material.

Current Controversies is also ideal for controlled research. Each anthology in the series is composed of primary sources taken from a wide gamut of informational categories including periodicals, newspapers, books, U.S. and foreign government documents, and the publications of private and public organizations. Readers will find factual support for reports, debates, and research papers covering all areas of important issues. In addition, an annotated table of contents, an index, a book and periodical bibliography, and a list of organizations to contact are included in each book to expedite further research.

Perhaps more than ever before in history, people are confronted with diverse and contradictory information. During the Persian Gulf War, for example, the public was not only treated to minute-to-minute coverage of the war, it was also inundated with critiques of the coverage and countless analyses of the factors motivating U.S. involvement. Being able to sort through the plethora of opinions accompanying today's major issues, and to draw one's own conclusions, can be a complicated and frustrating struggle. It is the editors' hope that Current Controversies will help readers with this struggle.

Introduction

> *"Once a center for economic, cultural, and intellectual development . . . the Middle East now lags behind much of the world economically and has become known for the spread of an anti-intellectual, fundamentalist version of Islam."*

Centuries ago, during a golden age of Islam that lasted approximately from A.D. 750 to 950, a vast Muslim empire covered much of the Middle East. Muslims at this time were leaders in world trade and known for their culture, philosophy, and scholarly advancements in science, math, engineering, and other intellectual areas. Arab merchants from the region traveled by camel caravans to distant lands to trade products such as cloth, pearls, livestock, paper, and sugar for metals, wood, foods, and other necessities that were scarce in Arab lands. In fact, the extensive trading activities of the Arabs rivaled those of the Chinese and were far more advanced than Europe's during this period of history. Once a center for economic, cultural, and intellectual development, however, the Middle East now lags behind much of the world economically and has become known for the spread of an anti-intellectual, fundamentalist version of Islam.

The reasons for the Middle East's decline are varied and are still debated by modern scholars. Over a period of many centuries, Arab trading activities were disrupted by events such as changes in leadership, an invasion of Arab lands by the Turks in the eleventh century that led to centuries of Turkish Ottoman rule, and the onslaught of the Crusades, a military effort by European Roman Catholics to recover the Holy Land from the Muslims. Later, advances in shipbuilding and seamanship eventually caused sea travel to displace land trade routes, and by the sixteenth century other regions such as Europe had eclipsed the Middle East as the leaders in world trade.

During recent times, the Middle East has come under the control of European and American powers, due largely to the discovery of massive amounts of oil in the region in the early twentieth century. This era began at the end of World War I in 1918, when Britain and France divided up the Ottoman Empire and set the borders of most modern Arab nations. The two European countries then installed a number of weak Arab governments, and for a period of several decades acted as colonial powers, controlling Arab economies while reaping the benefits of newly discovered oil resources. Since World War II, however, and particularly since the collapse of the Soviet Union in 1989, the United States has become the dominant power in the Middle East and the biggest defender of Western access to the region's oil.

During these last several decades, despite its massive oil resources, the Middle East has swelled in population but stagnated economically. Indeed, the region's population is expected to more than double by 2050 to about 649 million. Yet at the same time, the Middle East has declined in agricultural production and most types of trade. Oil now dominates the region's economic and political life. Because oil is the world's main energy source, it has made the region a crossroads for conflict between larger world powers and created deep divisions among local Arab and other Muslim peoples. In fact, oil has created a significant wealth gap in the region, making some lucky countries and individuals in the Middle East extravagantly wealthy but leaving many people impoverished and without hope. Oil-producing countries such as Saudi Arabia, Kuwait, and the United Arab Emirates are known around the world for their lavish oil wealth and their high standards of living, while countries without oil resources, such as Yemen, struggle to provide for their populations. The per capita average yearly income in the United Arab Emirates, for example, is twenty one thousand dollars, compared with only eight hundred dollars for Yemen. And even in richer Arab countries, there is a huge income and standard-of-living gap between wealthy ruling families and ordinary people.

Although some richer countries and populations are faring well, overall the Middle East region suffers from high unemployment (which ranges between 12 and 20 percent in many countries); a lack of housing, schools, and infrastructure; poor health care; a low number of exports and imports; and a generally sluggish economy. Especially in the areas of education and health care, the region lags behind much of the rest of the developing world. Women, in particular, have not been integrated into schools or workforces, largely because of religious and cultural ideas that instead encourage them to marry young and focus on raising families. And increased competition for scarce water resources prevents the development of agriculture and causes most countries in the region to import the bulk of their food.

The recent trend of globalization, typified by increased global trade as well as communication advances such as the Internet, has only left many parts of the Middle East further behind economically. Unlike many undeveloped countries in other parts of the world, most countries in the Middle East have failed to implement reforms or liberalize their trade rules to become part of this global trading system. At the same time, globalization has brought Internet access and global news to millions of people in the area, allowing them to see firsthand the huge disparities between their lives and those of comparatively rich Americans and the Arab ruling classes.

Some commentators suggest that the Middle East's lack of economic development and inability to provide bright futures for its young people may be an underlying cause of modern terrorism and conflict in the region. These critics suggest that young Arabs see Western countries like the United States exploit the region's resources and fill the coffers of Arab ruling classes while showing no concern for the millions of local people who receive no benefit from these riches. This exploitation, many people think, breeds deep resentment and hatred of the West that creates growing support for terrorist groups like al Qaeda and its violent goals of attacking American and Western targets. U.S. support of antidemocratic, authoritarian regimes in oil-producing countries such as Saudi Arabia may only add to the discontent, fortifying extremists who seek to overthrow these governments. According to this view, the quest of al Qaeda and other Islamic groups to reestablish Islamic rule may be rooted in a desire to return the Middle East to an era of economic prosperity similar to its golden age. Other experts disagree, arguing that poverty does not breed terrorism.

Whatever role it might play in creating unrest, economic inequality is only one of the problems that plague the Middle East. The authors in *Current Controversies: The Middle East* provide insight into the many other triggers for conflict in this troubled region.

CHAPTER 1

Current
CONTROVERSIES

Why Is the Middle East a Conflict Area?

The Middle East: An Overview

Subhash Kapila

Subhash Kapila is a former soldier and diplomat from India who writes extensively on foreign policy issues and strategic affairs for think tanks and professional journals. His writes a weekly column, Plain Speak, on foreign policy topics for the online magazine, Boloji.com.

The Middle East is the common appellation by which West Asia is better known and is the huge swathe of territory which lies between the Mediterranean Sea and the Indian Sub-continent. It is one of the most significant geo-strategic regions in the world in which the strategic interests of the global major powers intersect. Home to the world's largest deposits of oil and natural gas, the region has seen conflicts and tussles for control of these resources and the jostling for influence in the region.

Reason for Conflict

The Middle East region comprises predominantly Islamic nations with the exception of Israel. With the exception of Iran, the Islamic countries of the Middle East are ethnically Arab in composition. The emergence of Israel in 1948 as a new nation state in the Middle East firmament was hotly opposed politically and militarily by the Arab countries. This hostility lingers till today and is the main cause of conflict and confrontation.

Oil was used as a weapon by the Arab countries in the early 1970's to bring the Arab-Israel dispute to the fore. The oil prices were tripled and flush with their new found financial resources the Middle East countries undertook a massive modernization and up-gradation of their armed forces and thereby adding further conflictual contours to an already unstable region.

During the Cold War years, in terms of influence the Middle East was marked by a United States area of influence comprising oil-rich Arab monarchial states and a Soviet area of influence comprising the Arab Socialist radical regimes led by military officers mostly who had overthrown the monarchial regimes in their states. Both United States and the Soviet Union armed their protégé states heavily and the Middle East became one of the most heavily militarized regions of the world. In addition the United States was heavily militarizing the Shah regime in Iran as the pillar of its strategic configuration.

The Islamic Revolution in Iran in 1979 drastically changed the strategic picture ... [and] brought ... Islam as a politico-religious weapon.

To the externally generated conflict prone contours must also be added the domestic political, economic and social divides that characterized the region which in turn added turbulence to the conflicts and confrontation that distinguished the region. In the Arab monarchial countries allied to the United States the oil riches never percolated down to the masses fuelling discontent and radical tendencies. The Arab socialist states were not oil-rich and had to depend mostly on external economic aid. Resources for economic development were scarce due to high costs of military build-up and this again created discontent and social confrontation.

The Power of Islam

The Islamic Revolution in Iran in 1979 drastically changed the strategic picture in the Middle East. It brought into prominence with telling effect the power of Islam as a politico-religious weapon not only to overthrow despotic regimes but that such regimes despite their strong patronage from a superpower like the United States could also *be* overthrown. The

United States-Iran confrontation that originated in 1979 prevails even today with greater intensity with the eventuality of Iran acquiring nuclear weapons.

With the end of the Cold War and the disintegration of the Soviet Union the United States emerged as the global superpower with unmatched military superiority and with no countervailing power to restrain it. Ironically, along with it in tandem emerged the specter of the Middle East now becoming a region of conflict and confrontation with Islamist forces ranged against the United States in asymmetric warfare and global terrorism. 9/11 was the extreme manifestation of this fanatical Islamist confrontation with the United States.

The Middle East today seems to be engulfed in a vicious . . . onslaught by Islamist fundamentalist forces against the United States and the West.

A History of Perpetual Conflict

The Middle East has perpetually been in conflict and confrontation since the end of World War II. There have been four Arab-Israeli Wars, the Anglo-French Invasion of the Suez Canal, the Lebanon Wars, the eight year long Iran-Iraq War, the invasion of Kuwait by Iraq, the two Gulf Wars by the United States against Iraq and the many side show conflicts that interspersed these conflicts.

In 2007, the picture of the Middle East in terms of conflict and confrontation looks as dismal as ever. There is a virtual civil war in Iraq alongside the insurgency against the United States forces. There is an intense confrontation between the United States and Iran over the nuclear issue which could blow into full scale hostilities. Iran and Saudi Arabia can be said to be in a Cold War mode with a tussle to emerge as regional powers. Israel is besieged by Palestinian and Lebanese armed Islamic militias. Islamic militias are also battling American forces in Iraq. Al Qaeda is now making inroads into the Middle East with their leadership safely ensconced in Pakistan.

So what we are seeing today is not wars between the Arab nations and the United States but a host of armed militias of the Islamic world ranged against the United States, the West and Israel stretching from Lebanon to Afghanistan; that is the entire expanse of the Middle East. And to make matters worse none of the Arab nations allied to the United States seems to ... [be] making an effort to control this confrontation.

Conflict and confrontation today in the Middle East can be said to be acquiring the contours of a 'War of Civilizations' as visualized by [political scientist Samuel] Huntington. The Middle East today seems to be engulfed in a vicious conflict and onslaught by Islamist fundamentalist forces against the United States and the West. With such contours the conflict and confrontation in the Middle East presents the dismal prospects of being long drawn-out and vicious. Within the Middle East no sane voices or civil societies are visible which could advise or impose restraint on the armed Islamist militias or to curb terrorism of the Al Qaeda variety. The United States and the West therefore have a formidable challenge on their hands and ... any Middle East peace processes would have to be 'inclusivist' intiatives which may require co-opting Russia and China too.

U.S. Pursuit of Oil and Natural Gas Resources Creates Conflict in the Middle East

Michael T. Klare, interviewed by Julian Brookes

Julian Brookes is the editor of MotherJones.com, *the online version of* Mother Jones, *an independent, nonprofit magazine committed to social justice implemented through first-rate investigative reporting. Michael T. Klare is the Five College Professor of Peace and World Security Studies at Hampshire College in Amherst, Massachusettes.*

Welcome to the permanent global energy crisis. Though experts differ on when the precise moment of "peak oil" (also known as the end of cheap oil) will come, few deny that it's on the way. Already, supply is tightening, even as demand surges, pushing the price of oil (and gas at the pump) skyward. Increasingly, countries are scrounging the world for additional supplies and competing for a declining pool of essential petroleum, most of it located in politically unstable corners of the developing world—in the Middle East, Africa, Latin America, and Central Asia. In the coming years the United States, which consumes 25 percent of the world's oil, and whose economic and military might are utterly dependent on it, will increasingly be drawn into a geopolitical struggle over dwindling supplies with other "great powers," especially China. American foreign and military policy, already inextricably intertwined with energy imperatives, will be driven more and more by the need to keep oil flowing to the U.S.

The above is the broad argument of *Blood and Oil: The Dangers and Consequences of America's Growing Dependency on Imported Petroleum*, by Michael T. Klare. For all the periodic high-sounding talk of energy independence, he writes, Washington has in fact made little serious effort to wean the United States from oil. Instead, our government has recklessly set the nation up for more dependence, more U.S. military entanglements overseas, and, consequently, less security for Americans at home and abroad.

There *is* a way out of this—what Klare calls a "strategy for energy autonomy and integrity"—but it will take leadership from government and sacrifice from citizens, and some enlightened long-term thinking from both. Klare is the Five College Professor of Peace and World Security Studies at Hampshire College in Amherst, and author of *Resource Wars*, among other books. He's also a frequent contributor, via Tomdispatch, to MotherJones.com.

There's a growing panic . . . about the future availability of oil and natural gas, which are absolutely essential in modern industrial societies.

Julian Brookes: *You argue that in the 21st century resources rather than ethnic, civilizational, or religious differences will increasingly be at the root of conflict.*

Michael T. Klare: Yes. I think this is true both of internal and interstate conflicts. Two of the bloodiest wars under way in the world today—in Congo and Darfur—have arisen from the stress caused by rising population, a scarcity of resources, and climate change, which have exacerbated traditional ethnic differences, pushing people into conflict with one another. There are ethnic differences involved, of course, and I'd never say that a war is *exclusively* driven by resources, but they are a major factor.

As for international conflict, the focus is particularly on energy. I think there's a growing panic in the major industrialized countries about the future availability of oil and natural gas, which are absolutely essential in modern industrial societies. And this is causing the United States, Russia, China, and Japan and other large industrial countries to try to gain control over foreign sources of oil and natural gas, particularly in Africa, the Middle East and Central Asia. I wouldn't say we can expect *direct* conflict between these countries in the immediate future, but they are supporting local allies, often militarily, and this creates the conditions in which a local conflict can escalate into something very much bigger.

Oil from the Middle East is essential to the United States, and therefore we'll use any means necessary to protect it, including military force.

This is almost a reassertion of the great power politics of old.

Absolutely, I see this being very similar to the period before World War I, where you had a group of contending empires—the British, French, Prussian, Russian, Austro-Hungarian, and Ottoman empires—all competing with one another for control over colonies and the resources those colonies brought them. A lot of the skirmishing that led to World War I occurred in these colonial areas, in Africa and in the Balkans, and this triggered a war between them.

So resources will be at the core of much conflict, and oil in particular. What's special about oil?

Oil is essential for a modern, industrial society. It's unique, first of all, because it's the primary source, at 40 percent, of the world's entire supply of energy, and it's irreplaceable in the transportation field; it provides 98 percent of world transportation energy.

Oil is also essential for military operations. No other substance, no other raw material, is so vital for the prosecution of warfare, than petroleum. And the United States being the world's only global power, is totally dependent on petroleum. The Department of Defense is the world's leading petroleum consumer. And the U.S. couldn't play a military role in different areas like Iraq and Afghanistan without huge quantities of oil. So a shortage or disruption in oil would not only damage the U.S. economy; it would undercut American military supremacy.

For that reason, oil in the United States is treated as a *national security* matter, not just an economic one. No other substance has that character, such that the president of the United States has said—in this case it was Jimmy Carter in 1980—that oil from the Middle East is essential to the United States, and therefore we'll use *any means necessary* to protect it, including military force.

You argue that we've already entered a permanent energy crisis? What do you mean by that?

We are in a state of a permanent energy crisis, and it will last indefinitely—until there is a solution to it. And no solution right now is in sight, so this is a permanent feature of our landscape. It arises from several factors. One we've mentioned: U.S. dependence on oil for its economy and military power. The second problem is that the global supply of oil is going to decline because we've used up a good deal of the easy-to-get oil. We're going to reach a point in the not-too-distant future when it is impossible to keep increasing the daily supply. People call this the moment of "peak oil" production. There's debate about when that moment will arise, but there's no question that it's coming. Everybody is going to be scrounging the world looking for additional supplies and competing for a declining pool of essential petroleum. Making matters worse, most of the world's remaining pool of oil is in the developing world, in the Middle East, in Africa, in Latin America, and Central Asia, and these are areas that are inherently unstable. And so we're becoming more dependent and competing with other countries for access to a diminishing pool of oil in fundamentally dangerous areas. That's a sure recipe for disaster.

There was what you called 'a fork in the road' in 2001 where the [George W.] Bush administration, despite having explicitly acknowledged that there was some kind of an energy crisis, "chose dependency."

We had an energy crisis, remember, in 2000 and in 2001, with electricity black outs in California, natural gas shortages in the Mid West and oil shortages in the Eastern part of the country. And this was a major theme in the 2000 election. And President Bush said his highest priority—this was before 9-11, before terrorism became the focus—was to address the energy crisis. He said we need a fundamental change, a top-to-bottom review, and he gave the impression that he was ready to contemplate rather substantial innovations. But he picked *Dick Cheney*, an oil man, to run this review, and Cheney chose only to consult people in the oil industry, primarily Kenneth Lay and people from Enron. No environmentalists.

What they essentially decided—secretly, because the administration has refused to make public any of the minutes of these meetings—was to perpetuate the existing energy system for another 20 years at massive public expense, rather than to consider the proposals coming from the environmental community to shift very rapidly towards energy alternatives. And now, [in 2006] as a result of that decision, the United States is in worse shape than ever before. We're even more dependent on imported oil. No progress has been made in developing energy alternatives.

And Hurricane Katrina brought that fact into pretty stark relief, didn't it?

Yes, because Katrina destroyed or damaged the oil facilities in one of the most promising new areas for oil production, which is the deep waters of the Gulf of Mexico. Those facilities in the deep waters were hit the hardest by Katrina, and they have not recovered since. The more we look into the future we see that all the other potential sources for new oil are in dangerous areas, whether because of climate or the environment, or politically. And Katrina, I think, was a turning point in that it threw into relief the fragility of the international energy system, and it shows us that we can have no confidence that things are going to get better in the future.

The United States has to send troops all over the world to protect oil—not only in the Middle East, but in Latin America, Africa and Central Asia.

The Bush administration calculated in 2001 that a campaign to wean the country from oil dependency wasn't a political winner.

Right. In 1975 and 1976, we faced an energy crisis, President Carter told everyone they had to tighten their belts and lower the thermostat and wear sweaters. He wore a cardigan on a national TV speech! And at the time people found this to be too depressing and distasteful, and so they voted him out of office. So there is a kind of belief that the public is not willing to undertake any measures that would require them to change.

Do you see any sign of a shift on that score?

Yes, I do. I think, beginning with Katrina and continuing to the present—gaining momentum even—the public is now moving ahead of politicians. There are many signs, polling data in particular, that the public *does* grasp the magnitude of the problem and *is* now prepared to make sacrifices and changes. And this, I think, is going to have a significant political effect in the coming elections.

One possible response to the permanent energy crisis is to diversify, meaning getting oil from a range of different areas to reduce the dependency on oil from the Persian Gulf. But you don't buy that.

This was part of the strategy adopted by the administration in 2001. They recognized the U.S. would become more dependent on imports if we were going to continue to rely on oil as our main source of energy, but to try to reduce vulnerability to crisis in any one area they favored the strategy of diversification. The problem is that all the alternatives to the Middle East are just as dangerous. They include Africa, the Andean region of Latin America, Central Asia, North Africa— all pieces prone to corruption, internal warfare, and conflict. And so the logical conclusion of this strategy is what I call the globalization of the Carter doctrine, the notion that the United States has to send troops all over the world to protect oil—not only in the Middle East, but in Latin America, Africa and Central Asia. And that's the policy the administration has carried out.

And anyway, isn't it the case that no matter how much the U.S. diversifies, we'll still be largely dependent on Persian Gulf oil?

That's absolutely right, because nowhere else has that much oil. And even if the U.S. doesn't get its' own oil from the Persian Gulf, we're still dependent on Persian Gulf oil because that's the major source supply for Japan and Western Europe. If they weren't able to get more oil from the Persian Gulf, then they would be coming to the places that *we* rely on— Nigeria, Latin America and so on, and that would hugely increase the competition and the price. So, for world oil prices to remain relatively low—they seem high today, but they could get a lot, lot higher—is for the Persian Gulf to churn out more and more and more oil every year.

It's also hard to imagine that the U.S. would have gotten involved in Iraq if they didn't happen to have massive oil reserves.

Absolutely. But bear in mind that the invasion of Iraq was not an unprecedented event; it really was the natural extension of a conflict with Iraq that began on August 2, 1990, when Iraq invaded Kuwait and occupied Kuwait, which was a major oil supplier to the United States, and threatened Saudi Arabia, the leading foreign supplier to the United States. So when George Bush, Sr. announced U.S. intervention in the Persian Gulf conflict in 1990 it was explicitly to protect oil, the oil of Saudi Arabia. And that led to a massive deployment of American forces to the region, to the acquisition of more military bases, and later to the quarantine of Iraq. The invasion can't be separated from all of that broader conflict, which is a conflict, at its root, about *oil*—not just about the oil of Iraq, but about dominance of the entire Persian Gulf region.

You have to view Iran, like Iraq, as part of the large Persian Gulf region. Under U.S. policy—[enshrined in the Carter doctrine]—stability in the greater Persian Gulf region is essential to U.S. national security, because of its oil supplies, so anything that threatens stability in the Persian Gulf is a threat to America's national interests. That's how Iran is seen in Washington—as a potential threat to American dominance of the Persian Gulf. We're really talking about a geopolitical contest in which oil is the ultimate prize. That is the primary issue between the U.S. and Iran here—the power struggle over who will be dominant in this crucial region.

That having been said, Iran is believed to be the second largest producer of oil and the second leading producer of natural gas. Under the current U.S. policy, because of this power struggle, American oil companies can't do business with Iran. So I think the ultimate goal of the U.S. administration in Iran is regime change, to put into power a pro-Western government that will eliminate the strategic challenge to U.S. interests and, at the same time, allow the lifting of sanctions and allowing American oil companies to do business with Iran.

Any opinion on the chances of a military strike by the U.S.?

Knowing how the U.S. government has worked in the past, I imagine that President Bush has on his desk a national security game plan that has a host of options—Plan A, Plan B and Plan C, Plan D. They probably all have code names. But Plan A is to continue things as they are—diplomatic pressure. Plan

B, I think, is precise, limited attacks on Iranian nuclear weapons facilities, like the Israeli attack on the Osirak Reactor in Baghdad. Plan C would include covert operations aligned at stirring up a rebellion in Iran that would overthrow the clerical government. And Plan D would be more full-scale military operations. This is pure speculation on my part, but I'm sure planning like this is underway. . . .

The trends are pointing toward greater and deeper and more problematic U.S. involvement, often military involvement, in all sorts of parts of the world. Can we expect even more U.S. bases in these parts of the world, ever-closer military ties with these countries?

Yes to all of the above.

Water Is a Major Source of Conflict in the Middle East

Piers Moore Ede

Piers Moore Ede is a writer who lives in London.

O f all the resources we need as a species, water is the most important—it is, quite simply, the foundation of all life. While [oil] is essential for combustion engines and electricity generation, there are alternatives, albeit more expensive ones. For water, on the other hand, there are no alternatives. We cannot drink or irrigate our crops with anything else. And because many of the world's rivers and underground aquifers cross political boundaries, water is also one of the most likely causes of conflict.

Water Shortages in the Middle East

During a recent visit to Lebanon, it was suggested to me that the war in the Middle East is, among other things, a war for water. For most people, the Middle East is divided primarily along religious and ethnic lines. But if we look beneath the surface, a number of other issues play a strong part, not the least of which is the control of vital water sources in a region totally dependent on agriculture. The occupied territories are mainly valuable for the water they contain.

"If you stand on the southern border of Lebanon," says Caroll, an ecotour guide working out of Beirut, "you'll be struck by the fact that our side is dry while the Israeli side is green, lush, and well-irrigated. There are orchards, lawns, even swimming pools. And yet you are talking about a matter of a few feet in distance between our countries."

Clean water should be a basic human right. Yet by 2025, the UN predicts that nearly half the world's population will

Piers Moore Ede, "Fueling Tensions with Water: The Liquid Dimension to the Middle East Conflict," *Earth Island Journal*, vol. 18, winter 2004, pp. 46–48. Copyright 2004 Earth Island Institute. Reproduced by permission.

experience critical water shortages. And the Middle East, an already volatile region, has the lowest per capita water supply in the world. North Africa and the Middle East account for 6.3 percent of the world's population, but have just 1.4 percent of the world's renewable fresh water. [In 2004], Professor Boutros Boutros-Ghali, former Secretary General of the United Nations, reiterated the concern he first voiced in 1985. "The next war in the Middle East will be fought over water, not politics."

The Lebanese–Israeli Dispute over Water

[In 2003] tensions flared when Lebanon announced its intention to install a pump at the Wazzani Springs. The Springs run into the Hasbani River, which flows through Israel on its way to the Sea of Galilee; en route it feeds the fish farms of four kibbutzes [communal farms]. The sudden extra demand for water by the Lebanese in this area is not just because there has been less rainfall in the last few years. Since the Israeli retreat from the area in 2000, the Lebanese have been rebuilding villages that existed there before the conflict. People are returning home.

. . . the US has offered $500 million in aid to Lebanon, which would be used to build a water distribution facility in the South. The only catch is that Lebanon must first disarm the Hezbollah.

Israeli Prime Minister Ariel Sharon wasted no time in threatening swift military action if the pumping did not cease, accusing the Lebanese of "stealing" Israeli water supplies. The facts of the matter, however, are not so clear. The springs are fed by the Jordan River system, which is an international watershed. The Johnston Agreement of 1955 was drawn up for the specific purpose of allocating water rights to all four countries that feed off the Jordan system: Jordan, Israel, Lebanon, and Syria. Israel was granted the largest portion of the water. The Lebanese were granted 35 million cubic meters (mcm) per year. Due to the hostilities of the last few decades, they have taken barely more than 7 mcm per year. The new pump would have brought the total to 10–15 mcm.

The dispute took place during the buildup to war in Iraq, and George W. Bush was anxious to retain what little Arab support he had. American peacekeepers hurried to the scene where they cautioned both the Lebanese and the Israelis to use "restraint." But for the Lebanese, that restraint meant not supplying running water to a region desperately in need. Many villages are supplied with drinking and irrigation water by a single weekly truck.

Escalating Tensions

The Israelis ask why the Lebanese don't pump from the Litani, a much larger river, whose waters flow into the Mediterranean north of the frontier. But the Litani's water is heavily polluted and unfit for drinking. Building a water treatment plant would be a costly, time-consuming procedure. Why should they, say the Lebanese, when they have a right to use the Wazzani? So the construction continued, with each side making bolder and more belligerent threats. Israel began a nightly regimen of amplified wolf cries across the wire in order to upset pipeline workers. Apache gunships hovered just across the border.

On November 3, 2002, shortly after the pumping station started operation, Israeli jets made menacing passes overhead. The Shiite militant group Hezbollah sent armed men to protect pumping station workers. Asked by the *Jerusalem Post* whether the project would be considered a provocation for war by Israel, Prime Minister Sharon responded: "Israel will not allow the Hasbani to be diverted. I want to be very clear on this. And we are ready to deal with this issue."

Hezbollah responded to Sharon's threats with some of their own. Executive Committee member Hashem Safiedin said: "If they even think about using force to stop the Lebanese exploiting the waters of the Wazzani, we will cut their hands off."

The Lebanese are still pumping, though they have agreed to limit their take to drinking water, and not use the larger amounts required for badly needed irrigation. The latest development—spurred, no doubt, by the Bush administration's keenness to prevent any additional conflicts in the Middle East while it grapples with the situation in Iraq—is that the US has offered $500 million in aid to Lebanon, which would be used to build a water distribution facility in the South. The only catch is that Lebanon must first disarm the Hezbollah. Clearly, that is unlikely to happen.

A Global Problem

Whatever happens in this difficult situation, it is unlikely to be resolved in the near future and without sizeable concessions by both sides. Of paramount importance, though, is that the world's leaders heed these events as signifying a global problem. The World Water Development Report published [in 2004] suggests that our global water supply will drop by an average of a third per person over the next 20 years. Their optimum estimate for the situation in 2025 is that two billion people, throughout 48 countries, will face major water scarcity. It could, however, be as many as seven billion if major change is not implemented immediately.

"Water consumption has almost doubled in the last 50 years," says the report. "A child born in the developed world consumes 30 to 50 times the water resources of one in the developing world. Meanwhile water quality continues to worsen. . . . Every day, 6,000 people, mostly children under the age of five, die from diarrhoeal diseases." The future, for many parts of the world, looks bleak.

Israeli Violence Against Palestinians Creates Conflict in the Middle East

Jeremy Salt

Jeremy Salt is an associate professor in the Department of Political Science at Bilkent University in Ankara, Turkey.

In the form of suicide bombers striking in [the Israeli cities of] Jerusalem, Haifa, Tel Aviv and Netanya, the chickens are coming home to roost with blood-drenched wings. There are echoes here of the barrel bombs the Zionists [militant Jews] rolled into Arab markets in the 1940s, or the bombing of the King David Hotel [by Jewish militants seeking to oust the British from Israel]. In blood and fire was the state born, in blood and fire has it lived, and in blood and fire is it still gripped. The state is now in the hands of extremists and there is apparently no-one willing or able to restrain them; neither the European Union nor the United Nations nor the United States. . . .

Israeli Military Tactics

[In 2002] Arab heads of state and foreign ministers were meeting in Beirut to discuss the Saudi peace 'initiative'. This contained nothing that had not been said, sought or demanded over the past three decades; but was interesting because it came from the Saudis, whose last high-profile peace initiative (the Fahd plan) was put forward while the Israelis were attacking Lebanon in 1982. As was the case then, the Saudis now feel directly threatened by the tempest beginning to blow

Jeremy Salt, "Armageddon in the Middle East? The Roots of the Current Middle-East Conflict Were Laid Long Before Israel Was Founded. The Last, Best Hope for a Just Peace Is That the Israeli People Will Come to Terms With the Problematic History of Zionism," *Arena Magazine*, April–May 2002, pp. 5–8. Copyright 2002 Arena Printing and Publications Pty. Ltd. Reproduced by permission.

up over Palestine. The Beirut Arab summit was typically acrimonious. It was characterised by non-attendances, boycotts and walkouts, but at the end all those present endorsed the Saudi plan. It offered Israel recognition and normalisation in return for the withdrawal from all territory seized in the 1967 war and acknowledgement of the Palestinian right of return. This is not the same as demanding that all Palestinians be allowed to return to their homeland, but recognising the right would at least be a starting point for negotiations.

The Palestinians are now using every weapon to defend themselves and strike back at [Israeli] settlers.

The very next day the Arabs had [then Israeli prime minister Ariel] Sharon's answer—a column of tanks and troop carriers rolling into Ramallah [the headquarters of the Palestinian government] where they broke through the walls of [the Palestinian president Yasser] Arafat's presidential compound. Loudhailers [bullhorns] were used to summon all males between fourteen and fifty to the nearest mosque or school for interrogation and whatever else might follow. The victims of the soldiers roaming through the streets included men, women and children and Palestinian policemen who in no way can be said to be part of Sharon's 'terrorist infrastracture', but then neither were the civilians massacred at [the Palestinian cities of] Sabra and Shatila in the name of hunting down terrorists. In Arafat's compound the bodies of five men were seen strewn in one room. They had been executed with a single bullet to the head, according to the Palestinians. The morgues in Palestinian towns across the West Bank [were] filled with bodies. Others could not be retrieved because of the fighting and the wounded could not be taken to hospital because the Israelis blocked the passage of ambulances. Arafat remained alive but [then U.S. secretary of state] Colin Powell had to ask Sharon not to kill him. That Sharon would prefer him dead he himself had made clear, and with fighting going on in the next room it remained possible that the Palestinian leader would be killed accidentally or while 're-sisting arrest'. Sharon's offer of a one-way ticket into exile was contemptuously rejected. Having dealt with Ramallah first, hundreds of tanks and thousands of soldiers were sent into other cities. In Bethlehem hundreds of people sheltered in churches—not just suspected 'militants', but terrified men, women and children. The destruction of the Palestinian Authority, the suppression of the people and the reoccupation of the land, all of which Sharon had been working on since he became Prime Minister, was soon well underway. When the [U.N.] Security Council called on Israel to withdraw it simply broadened its operation. George [W.] Bush criticised the Israelis, but said he understood why they were doing what they had to do. In other words Israel was free to stay in the territories as long as it liked. . . .

The Palestinians are now using every weapon to defend themselves and strike back at settlers and the civilian population of the country whose government is responsible for the killing of their civilians. It was the suicide bomber vs the tank, the sniper and the Apache helicopter. Sharon's attempt to humiliate Arafat backfired immediately. Under the Israeli onslaught his people rallied behind him as never before. In Arab eyes this was vintage Israel.

Israel Created the "Palestinian Problem"

The 'Palestinian problem' is still with us . . . [but] again was Israel trying to solve it in time honoured fashion it is long past time to stop calling it the 'Palestinian problem'. There was no problem until the British came along and created it, and since 1948 the central problem in the Middle East has been Israel's refusal to comply with international law. There is not one war between itself and the Arabs that it has not started directly or indirectly. The 'declaration of independence' of

1948 was the uprising of settler minority against the indigenous land-owning majority. In 1956 it was the 'tripartite conspiracy' with Britain and France against Egypt. In 1967 it was the attack of Egypt and Syria. It was sold to the world as a 'pre-emptive strike', but in fact was a war of agression planned by [then Israeli defense minister] Moshe Dayan with the intention of bringing down [Egyptian president Gamal Abdul] Nasser, destroying Arab military capacity and acquiring more land. In 1973 it was Israel's refusal to withdraw from occupied Sinai that brought on the October War. In 1978 it was the invasion of Lebanon and in 1982 an even bigger attack on Lebanon. In between these events there have been assassinations and military strikes resulting in the deaths of large numbers of civilians. No attempt has ever been [made] to punish Israel for its violent behavior. As a result the problem has simply worsened year by year and decade by decade. Is it any wonder that Sharon thinks he can get away with murder again?

Retention of the land is the real point of . . . the historical, territorial and ideological war waged against the Palestinians.

Squandered Opportunities for Peace

Yet since the 1970s Israel could have had peace simply by holding out its hand and agreeing to comply with a minimalist interpretation of international law. The Arabs never wanted Israel amongst them, but since the 1970s at the latest they had resigned themselves to its existence. Egypt and Jordan signed peace treaties and have stuck to them ever since, despite the most egregious Israeli provocations in Lebanon and elsewhere. It was the Palestinians and not Israel or the United States who began working towards a two-state solution nearly thirty years ago. In the early 1990s they and the Israelis finally entered into a formal peace process which ended up in the junkyard of lost opportunities because Israel used it to demand even more from the Palestinians than they had already conceded.

Behind the rhetoric of peace every Israeli prime minister maintained the tempo of land expropriation and settlement expansion. [Former Israeli prime minister] Ehud Barak was as bad as any of them. There was no withdrawal, but redeployment, with Israeli tanks and troops surrounding the Palestinians in their autonomous scraps of territory. There were not fewer settlers after the 'peace process' began but more. The 'core issues' were all put off until Barak needed something to take to the people ahead of prime ministerial elections in 2000 that he seemed bound to lose. The argument that he and Arafat were an inch away from a settlement during talks brokered by [U.S. president] Bill Clinton at Camp David is a complete self-serving delusion. They were nowhere near the finishing line. If the talks had not broken down over Jerusalem they would have broken down over Israel's refusal to take legal and moral responsibility for the plight of the refugees. They were certainly going to break down. Yet the line that 'we made a generous offer which those ingrates refused' has been transformed into another weapon in the armory of the Israeli propagandist.

Land Is the Issue

Through this period the Israeli peace movement refused to draw the logical conclusions from the facts being created on the ground before also grasping at the generous offer—ungrateful response interpretation. The peace process was being [aborted] because no Israeli government was prepared to concede what was necessary for peace—a halt to settlement activity and a commitment to full withdrawal from the occupied territories that would have still left Israel with 78 per cent of Palestine. Abba Eban, the Israeli Foreign Minister of the 1960s and 1970s, was fond of saying that the Palestinians never lost an opportunity to lose an opportunity. It is a line that is still used against the Palestinians; but in reality it was Israel that squandered all the opportunities placed before it. Now it is the Saudi peace initiative that has been contemptuously tossed aside in favor of a crushing assault on the Palestinians which will break the people and enable Israel to remain in possession of the bulk if not all of the West Bank. To many Israelis reoccupation makes no sense. To Sharon and the settlers it does. Retention of the land is the real point of this fresh stage of the historical, territorial and ideological war waged against the Palestinians for the last century.

The Israelis are stuck in a trap of their own making . . . which can only raise questions about Israel's capacity to survive in the Middle East.

It was under the slogan of 'a land without people for a people without land' that Zionism first took root. It was no more true than it was true that Palestine was a desert which the Zionists made bloom. Large parts of it were very fertile. The oranges of Jaffa were famous around the world. Palestinian barley went into the making of Scotch whiskey. Wheat fields stretched along the coastal littoral as far south as Gaza. The peasant population had no intention of moving off the land and for the most part the owners had no intention of selling it. By the 1940s the Zionist colonial agencies had been able to acquire by legal purchase no more than 6 or 7 per cent. Clearly the land could only be acquired by taking it. The people were another problem. The idea of 'transfer' was there from the start: What would be necessary to establish a Jewish state in a land that was not Jewish was rarely talked about openly, but some did not mince words. Vladimir Jabotinsky was one of them. The founding figure of 'revisionist' Zionism, which still holds that the Land of Israel falls on both sides of the River Jordan, Jabotinsky wrote of the need to set up an 'iron wall' between the Zionist settlers and the Palestinians.

He knew that they would never agree to the implantation of a Jewish state on their land. It would have to be created over their heads. Asher Ginsburg—writing under the pen name of Ahad Ha'am—was someone else who was free of delusions but reached different conclusions. Early in the twentieth century he travelled to Palestine and saw for himself that the land was already occupied. For him the road taken by the Zionists was leading not to an iron wall but a grievous injustice. Others talked of a bi-national state; but Zionism was all about a Jewish state and that was not a project for the squeamish.

With the help of the British and the Americans the state came into existence. The Palestinians fled or were expelled. There was no need for a central order. The Zionist leadership did not want them there and many commanders in the field accurately picked up the signals. Having driven out the Palestinians in a bout of what would now be called ethnic cleansing, and having acquired three quarters of Palestine by 1949, David Ben Gurion—Israel's first prime minister—waited for the opportunity to take the rest. That came in 1967. From the moment of its creation Israel lived under the necessity of obliterating the Palestinians as a military and historical presence. Their rights could not be acknowledged or redressed. Yet they had not disappeared. They were living over the borders of neighboring countries . . . and because Palestine was an Arab cause, war had to follow war. The Palestinians were the living reminder of a sin that could not be admitted.

Desperation and Suicide Bombings

Thus the Israelis are stuck in a trap of their own making. Unable to let go and release themselves as well as the Palestinians they have continued on a path which can only raise questions about Israel's capacity to survive in the Middle East. It has made itself intolerable by the violence of its actions over the past five decades. These have largely been smothered by the Western media, but the facts are all there for anyone who wants to take a close look at the record. The current brutal campaign against the Palestinians, borne of a wave terrorism provoked by Ariel Sharon so that he would have the pretext to do what he is now doing, reads only like the latest instalment. Even Jewish writers acknowledge that Israel has become an engine of death and destruction in the Middle East. Not a year has passed without Israel giving free rein to its aggressive impulses. It has humiliated the Palestinians of the West Bank and Gaza for the past thirty-five years. It was not until the intifada [uprising] of 1987 that they finally rose up against occupation. Few weapons were used. This was an uprising of young men—the shabab—throwing stones at heavily armed troops and tanks, but many of them were killed nevertheless. In the early 1990s Palestinians welcomed the onset of the 'peace process'. Most of them accepted Arafat's word that it would result in the end of the Israeli presence in the territories and the establishment of a Palestinian state with its capital in East Jerusalem. He was wrong; and with 1500 people being killed in the territories since the beginning of the Aqsa intifada [in 2000] the Palestinians have finally reached a point of nihilistic desperation. The suicide bombings are shocking, but they cannot be separated from more than three decades of occupation and the murderous policies pursued by the state at the direction of Ariel Sharon. He has deliberately set out to provoke violence in the territories. He has killed and assassinated even in times of quiet. He has done this knowing that suicide bombings would follow. Yet even now it is the Palestinians who are being singled out for blame. The delusion now being fed into the American media by [*New York Times* columnist] Thomas Friedman and others is that the suicide bombers are a threat to civilisation and that they are acting not out of desperation but strategic choice. Well, perhaps it is a strategic choice borne out of desperation. . . .

The Fury with Israel

The climate across the Arab world has plunged back four decades. Having watched the battering of Lebanon and the killing of young stone-throwers in the intifada of the 1980s the people of the Arab world are now seeing a fresh cycle of brutal images being transmitted from Palestine by Al Jazeera television station twenty-four hours a day. There is fury with Israel. There have been massive demonstrations in every capital and demands for action of some sort—a severance of relations with both Israel and the United States—and it is surely only a matter of time before their demands have to be met unless Arab governments are themselves to fall.

Israel's long-term capacity to survive in the Middle East has never been more in doubt. Its government is in the hands of extremists. They may yet set off the war that Israel cannot win. It is now up to Israelis and Jews [worldwide] who are horrified by what is going on to take collective action. Some of them are already doing just this. They need full support. If they cannot launch a revolt that deflects Israel from the path Sharon has chosen and puts the country on a path that leads unambiguously to peace, another deadly collision between Israel and the Arabs seems inevitable. The chance is still there. The Arab states do not want war. Israel's military might alarms them. They are not ready yet to embrace Israel. They are still ready to accept it but time is running out.

Continuing Palestinian Terrorism Against Israel Creates Conflict in the Middle East

Mortimer B. Zuckerman

Mortimer B. Zuckerman is the editor in chief of U.S. News & World Report, *a weekly newsmagazine. He is also chairman and copublisher of the* New York Daily News.

Eleven months ago, Israel withdrew from every last inch of the Gaza Strip. The Israelis dismantled all military bases, destroyed all their settlements, turned over functioning greenhouses that could employ 4,000 people, expelled all 7,500 Israeli settlers—all at a huge financial and political cost. Prime Minister Ariel Sharon even went a step further, declaring the lines that divide Israel from Gaza an international frontier, making Gaza the first independent Palestinian territory ever.

Everyone hoped then that the Palestinians would show the world what they could achieve with freedom as a template for a future independent state. Alas, they have shown us all too well. Not one day of peace has followed since then. The pattern was set on the very day of Israel's pullout. Palestinian militants fired rockets from Gaza into Israeli towns on the other side of the border, targeting innocent civilians living in the pre-1967 Israel recognized by the international community. The final straw came with the Hamas attack that killed two Israeli soldiers and resulted in the kidnapping of a third. Inspired by the rhetorical threats of Iran's incendiary president, Mahmoud Ahmadinejad, Hezbollah—like Hamas, another Iranian proxy—attacked Israel from the north, killing eight Israeli soldiers and abducting two more, and then began raining rockets down onto Israeli civilians.

Mortimer B. Zuckerman, "From Bad to Worse," *U.S. News & World Report*, vol. 141, July 24, 2006, pp. 59–60. Copyright 2006 U.S. News and World Report, L.P. All rights reserved. Reprinted with permission.

Nature's Law

The Palestinians are giving the lie to virtually every scenario so hopefully envisaged by their friends, including Israeli supporters of disengagement. They failed to begin building schools, roads, and hospitals; they made no effort to turn Gaza into a thriving state, nor did they create villages of their own out of the settlements the Israeli government forced its settlers to abandon. They vandalized the greenhouses not once, but twice. They elected a radical Islamic Hamas government; they breached the border with Israel, permitting the smuggling of huge quantities of weapons and creating new bases for terrorism.

Not only did Hamas fail to become more moderate; Fatah and the Palestinians became even more radicalized, moving closer to Hamas's extremist position, choosing to interpret Israel's voluntary evacuation not as a gesture of peace but as a victory for the armed struggle. Terrorism in Gaza flourished, tunnels were dug, more weapons were imported, militants trained, more Kassam rockets were produced and fired at Israel.

Who can doubt the right—indeed, the duty—of a government to defend its citizens against random attacks?

At first, the Israelis tried nonlethal deterrence—diplomatic warnings, then sonic booms from fighter jets to remind the Gazans that Israel has the power to retaliate. Those failed. It was a sad demonstration of the truth in the metaphor that in the Middle East the law of nature prevails—an animal perceived as weak invites only attack. The Israelis fell back on targeted assassinations against the terrorist leaders—exactly what America did against Abu Musab Zarqawi in Iraq, despite the risk that innocents might be killed because the terrorists hide among civilians, moral shields for immoral men.

Some apologists suggest that Israel should ignore the Palestinian rockets because they are puny and erratic. That's easy to say from an armchair, but every one of the rockets fired into urban areas is intended to kill or maim as many Israeli civilians as possible. The Israeli town of Sderot lost 13 people to Palestinian rocket fire, and a third of the children are said to suffer from post-traumatic stress disorder. Now, Palestinian militants have begun firing longer-range rockets that have reached larger cities like Ashkelon, where 115,000 Israelis live.

The last thing Israel wanted to do was get involved again in Gaza, much less in Lebanon but Hamas and Hezbollah gave it no choice. Who can doubt the right—indeed, the duty—of a government to defend its citizens against random attacks? Who would doubt the U.S. response if rockets were raining from across the Mexican border into American cities, or if Canadian forces simultaneously killed and kidnapped Americans on U.S. soil? And who but Israel would be shipping foodstuffs, medicines, and chlorine containers for purifying drinking water to avoid a humanitarian crisis in Gaza? Could you imagine the allies sending foodstuffs and medicines to Germany during World War II? Perversely, the terrorist organizations are focusing terrorist acts on the very border crossings that are Gaza's lifelines. Why is Hamas doing this? To claim there is a humanitarian crisis in Gaza, as a way of forcing Israel to relinquish its efforts to find its abducted infantryman.

Israel has several objectives. First, it wants to reassert the power of its deterrence so that Hamas and Hezbollah know that terrorist violence will be met with ever more painful and far-reaching responses. Israel intends to make it crystal clear that kidnapping simply does not pay. Israeli intelligence has already detected 20 new kidnapping plots, with more undoubtedly to come. The Hamas government may wear suits and ties during the day but, in effect, wears black balaclavas at night. Dr. Jekyll may offer a cease-fire, but it is only a tactical pause for Mr. Hyde to rebuild for more war. The Hamas menace is not confined to Israel, for it is now welcoming other Islamic terrorist organizations, including al Qaeda and Hezbollah. The latter has already undermined the independence of the Lebanese government, and, indeed, is now a part of that government.

The core of the Israeli-Palestinian dispute stems not from Israel's unwillingness to compromise but from . . . the desire among Palestinians to eliminate Israel.

But what about Mahmoud Abbas, the pacific-sounding hope of the West? Yes, what of Mr. Abbas? Sadly, what we have witnessed is his utter failure to influence the Hamas government. He has failed to honor the pledge he gave Israeli officials to muster the forces for a house-to-house search for the abducted soldier. That he has folded to Hamas is evidenced by his agreement to a version of the so-called prisoners' document. It is not a basis for peace talks but a step toward war. It is a dramatic pullback from Fatah's previous position because it reopens the most vital questions about Israel's right to exist (which is explicitly rejected by the Hamas negotiators) and endorses terrorism and violence. It means that both Hamas and Fatah are equally committed to Israel's annihilation. Now that Fatah is seeking to outflank Hamas on the side of radicalism, it is no surprise that Israelis feel they do not have a partner for peace. Abbas's willingness to sign it should open the eyes of the world to the fact that he is no moderate and no potential peacemaker.

Code Words

Soon Israel will also have to confront the political challenge of a modified version of this "prisoners' manifesto" signed by Hamas and Abbas. Again, it is not really about peace with Israel; it is about ending the civil war between the Palestinian factions. The language of the document is confrontational, not compromising. It does not call for an end to terrorism against the Israelis, only an end to violence among the Palestinians. It repudiates the framework for peace negotiated by years of effort, specifically U.N. Resolution 242. It demands all territory captured by Israel in the 1967 defensive war. And even if that were conceded, which it is not, the document does not indicate that the Palestinians would then withdraw their claims to Israel's pre-1967 territory.

The Oslo accord—and the four-power road map agreement—called for an end to terrorism. This, instead, is a manifesto for terrorism. It does not require that the Palestinian Authority dismantle terrorism but just the opposite. It calls for continuing violence and for "popular resistance" against the Israeli occupation "in all its forms, places and policies," and "by all means," language long recognized as code for terrorism and as legitimizing the murder of Israelis. Nor does it restrict terrorism to the West Bank but only suggests that terrorism be focused in the West Bank, without precluding Palestinians from carrying out terrorist acts against Israel inside its pre-1967 borders.

Most critically, it advocates the right of return for some 4 million Palestinian refugees, as they define themselves today, the descendants of the 700,000 Arabs who fled during the 1948 war primarily at the behest of their own leaders. These refugees, under the new Palestinian manifesto, are now proposed to be returned to pre-1967 Israel, virtually putting the Jews into a minority in their own country—the very situation that the United Nations ruled out in deciding the original partition of Palestine.

The Palestinians' Desire to Eliminate Israel

Tragically, this document and the violence in Gaza have undermined the domestic support for the main program of Prime Minister Ehud Olmert (whom Hezbollah leader Hassan Nasrallah compared, unhelpfully, to [post–WWI British prime minister] Neville Chamberlain). That program—known as re-alignment—contemplated a dramatic withdrawal from roughly 90 percent of the West Bank. Today, 49 percent of the Israeli public opposes the realignment plan and only 38 percent supports it. It is clear that Israeli withdrawals and concessions have brought about not Palestinian moderation but just the opposite. It is equally clear that the proposed realignment of the West Bank's borders will now simply create a new battle line, just as the disengagement in Gaza created new battle lines. A withdrawal from the West Bank would put Hamas within range of Israel's main population centers and infrastructure, raising the fear that a rocket launched from the West Bank could hit the country's most densely populated areas, like Jerusalem, Tel Aviv, and Ben-Gurion airport. Israel cannot even begin to contemplate exposing its citizens to such peril. It will have to review its concept of the strongest defensive line.

It is more clear than ever that the core of the Israeli-Palestinian dispute stems not from Israel's unwillingness to compromise but from the nature of its adversary; and that the desire among Palestinians to eliminate Israel is too powerful, the adherence to violence too pervasive, to overcome. Most fair-minded observers share the Israeli conclusion that there is no Palestinian partner for peace. As the leading Egyptian paper, *Al-Ahram*, pointed out: "The Palestinians must be aware by now that they can no longer count on Arab help, economically, politically, or militarily. . . . Arab nations have had enough . . . of the slogans and rhetoric that have gotten us nowhere. . . . The Palestinians have lost Arab backing both on the official and nonofficial levels." And the CEO [chief executive officer] of the Arab News Agency Al Arabiya wrote, "Was the result worth all the damage it caused?"

The Middle East equation today could hardly be more stark or depressing. It reveals once again that Hamas and the Palestinians, now joined by Hezbollah, armed and financed by

Iran, wish to get rid of Israel. This will be a "long war" in which victory will be the culmination of a series of unavoidable catastrophes.

Islamic Extremism Causes Terrorist Violence in the Middle East

Paul Marshall

Paul Marshall is a senior fellow at the Center for Religious Free-dom, a project of Freedom House, a nonprofit organization that promotes freedom and democracy around the world. Marshall is also author of several books, including Islam at the Crossroads *(2002) and* God and the Constitution: Christianity and American Politics *(2002).*

Osama bin Laden's November 12 [2002] audiotape claimed that one reason for the brutal bombings in Bali ... was Australia's role in protecting East Timor and allowing it to separate from Indonesia's clutches. Typically, most analysts ignored this. The *Washington Post* even printed the relevant paragraph with this section missing, and with no ellipses to indicate its absence. This continues a pattern in which our media and political leaders ignore the forthright and articulate religious motives and ideology that drive al Qaeda and its allies. We are engaged in a war in which we resolutely ignore our enemies' stated goals.

Religious Terrorists

On September 11, [2001,] we were attacked by explicitly religious terrorists who said their prayers before going out to slaughter infidels. The movement they represent consistently outlines its goals through a plethora of books, websites, and videos, and gives a clear and articulate theology and view of history to justify and explain its actions. Bin Laden's 1998 *al Jazeera* [an Arabic news network] interview stressed this point:

Paul Marshall, "This War We're In: Taking Extremist Islam Seriously," *National Review Online*, November 26, 2002. Copyright © 2002 by National Review, Inc., 215 Lexington Avenue, New York, NY 10016. Reproduced by permission.

"There are two parties to the conflict: World Christianity, which is allied with Jews and Zionism, led by the United States, Britain, and Israel. The second party is the Islamic world." His 1998 merger with Egypt's Islamic Jihad formed the "World Islamic Front for Holy war against Jews and Crusaders," al Qaeda's real name, and he has described President [George W.] Bush as fighting under the "sign of the cross."

Al Qaeda's manual begins by recalling "the fall of our orthodox Caliphates [regions ruled by Islamic leaders] on March 3, 1924." Bin Laden's November 3, 2001, videotape proclaims, "Following World War I, which ended more than 83 years ago, the whole Islamic world fell under the Crusader banner. . . ." Their grievance, continually expressed, is the collapse of the Islamic world in the face of "Christendom," a collapse that can only be explained by Muslims' apostasy from Islam and only be reversed by returning to their version of Islam.

Hence al Qaeda and a network of extremist groups from Algeria to the Philippines consistently fight to impose their version of Islam on Muslims and, then, the rest of the world. They want a restored caliphate in which each country will submit to their version of Islamic sharia law. The Taliban wanted a Caliphate in Afghanistan, Uzbekistan's IMU in Central Asia, the Philippines' Abu Sayyaf and Indonesia's Jamaah Islamiya and Laskar Jihad in southeast Asia. Al Qaeda wants one for the whole world.

America's Failure to See Religious Motives

Yet in fighting these enemies we ignore these clear goals and filter their acts through a grid of western nostrums about alienation, economics, and the Middle East. We are told that al Qaeda's primary grievance is America, "the West," or freedom, or the plight of the Palestinians. But though al Qaeda has made it crystal clear that, in its own view, it is attacking, inter alia, Christians, whom it calls "crusaders," as well as Jews (and Hindus and Buddhists), American analysts, inside and outside the government, insist that its agenda is not religiously based but is simply anti-American.

America has become a focus of Islamist rage because . . . we stand in their way, thwart their intentions, and defeat their fighters.

Thus when, in August [2002], newly acquired bin Laden videotapes explicitly denounced "crusaders and Jews," CNN claimed that he was really targeting "the United States and the West," while CBS described his foes as "Americans," and the Associated Press asserted, without argument, that "Bin Laden has used the term 'crusaders' to refer to Westerners."

In September [2002], after the latest massacre of Pakistani Christians, in Taxila, Pakistan's center of Christianity since the second century, the *New York Times* called it an assault on "western targets," and Reuters headlined "Pakistan attack seen aimed at West, not Christians." Meanwhile, the attackers themselves said they "planned to kill Christians" and that they "killed the nonbelievers." In October [2002], the statement claiming credit for attacking an oil tanker off Yemen referred to a "crusader oil tanker." Despite this explicit religious reference to al Qaeda's purported Christian enemies, the *Washington Post* declared that they were opposed to the U.S. and have "often referred to the United States as 'crusaders.'" This attempt to equate crusaders with the United States is especially confusing since the tanker in question was French.

The Oct[ober] 12 [2002] bombing in Bali was also described by the media as directed at "the West," though it took place in Indonesia's only Hindu majority territory and coincided exactly with bombings on the Philippine consulate in Manado, a Christian area hundreds of miles away. Al Qaeda affiliates in Indonesia had already orchestrated the bombing of 36 Christian schools and churches in Indonesia during Christmas 2000, while its allies have massacred thousands of Christians in eastern Indonesia, the latest assault being the August 12 destruction of the Christian village of Sepe.

The November 12 [2002] bin Laden audiotape says that Australian victims were picked partly because of Australia's "despicable effort to separate [Catholic] East Timor" from Indonesia, thus undermining the hoped-for Southeast Asian Islamic state. Meanwhile, in the Philippines itself, Abu Sayyaf continues to massacre local Christians.

Similar tales can be told of the world's bloodiest conflict, in Sudan; of the slaughter of over 100,000 moderate Muslims by extremists in Algeria; of attacks on Hindus in Bangladesh, on Buddhists in Thailand, and on Hindus and Buddhists in Afghanistan; of the over six thousand dead in the conflict over the introduction of Islamic sharia law in Nigeria; of the Chechens' release of the Muslims amongst their Russian hostages in Moscow; and of attacks on Jews throughout the world. The largest death tolls from Islamist extremism do not occur in America or the West or Israel, but in Sudan, Algeria, and Indonesia.

America as Target

America has become a focus of Islamist rage because, when the terrorists seek to wreak their havoc around the world, whether in Israel, Pakistan, Malaysia, Indonesia, or Afghanistan, we stand in their way, thwart their intentions, and defeat their fighters. We also undercut their beliefs by urging the equality of women and individual and religious freedom. They are rendered impotent in all but death as long as American military might and American cultural power stands in their way.

Now, as Islamist terrorists repeat endlessly, their strategic goal must now be to make the United States retreat so that they can achieve Islamist rule elsewhere. Thus the chief demand of the November letter, ostensibly from al Qaeda, is that America end its support of those throughout the world who fight radical Islam: "Leave us alone or expect us in Washington and New York."

What does this mean for our current war against extremist Islam? First, that we are not fighting merely "terrorist" groups but a worldwide Islamist insurgency. Second, that our enemies are not driven simply by opposition to U.S. policy on Israel or the Middle East. They must be faced as an aggressive, expansionist, global ideological movement with its sights set also on Africa and Asia.

Third, the attacks on America are explicitly designed to strike fear in us in order to keep us from interfering with Islamist attempts to impose their will throughout the world. Hence any American withdrawal from conflict with extremist Islam, whether in the Middle East or Asia, will not guarantee peace and harmony. It will be a victory for Islamist terrorism, the fulfillment of their first strategic goal, and a prelude to expanded attacks elsewhere.

Islamic Sectarianism Increases the Risk of Conflict in the Middle East

Vali Nasr

Vali Nasr is a professor at the Naval Postgraduate School and an adjunct senior fellow at the Council on Foreign Relations, a think tank that focuses on international affairs. He is also the author of the 2006 book The Shia Revival: How Conflicts Within Islam Will Shape the Future.

The most significant development in the Middle East today is the rise of sectarian conflict. This is a process that has begun in Iraq, but it will not end there. In Iraq it has become the single most important determinant of that country's future. However, it has already spread beyond Iraq, threatening stability in Lebanon as it shapes regional alignments and the regional balance of power.

The Shia Revival

The rise of sectarianism is an outcome of the Shia [sect of Islam] revival that followed the fall of the Saddam Hussein regime in Iraq. The war broke down the Sunni [the other main sect of Islam] minority regime that had ruled that country for decades and empowered Shias, producing the first Arab Shia government in history and setting in motion a region-wide Shia revival. What began in Iraq quickly translated into a regional political dynamic as Shias everywhere looked to Iraq with hope for positive changes in their own countries.

In the wake of regime change in Iraq, the Shia have made their mark on regional politics. From Lebanon to the Persian Gulf, through peaceful elections and bloody conflicts, the Shia are making their presence felt. Shia politics were initially supportive of developments in Iraq. Senior Iraqi Shia leaders endorsed the political system the United States introduced to Iraq. Iraqi elections also received support from Iranian and Lebanese Shia religious leaders. Following the elections, Shias joined the American-backed government in Baghdad, and Shias joined the new Iraqi security forces in droves. Post-Saddam Iraq presented an opportunity for creating stable relations between the United States and Iraqi Shias and, by extension, with the Shia populations across the region.

Shias have been by and large an invisible political force, excluded from power whether in the majority or minority.

The History of Shiism

Shiism split off from Sunnism in the seventh century over a disagreement about who the Prophet Muhammad's legitimate successors were. Over time, the two sects developed their own distinct conception of Islamic teachings and practices much as Catholicism and Protestantism have in Christianity since the medieval period. Shias are a minority of 10–15 percent of the world's 1.3 billion Muslims.

The overwhelming majority of Shias live in the arc from Lebanon to Pakistan—some 140 million people in all. They account for about 90 percent of Iranians, 65 percent of Iraqis, 40–45 percent of Lebanese, and a sizable portion of the people living in the Persian Gulf region (and around the region in East Africa, India, and Tajikistan). There are small Shia communities in southern and western Africa, South and North America, and Europe—mostly migrants. Iran is today the largest Shia country, followed by Pakistan. Most Shias live from Iran to the east, where Arab Shias constitute only a minority of the faith. However, importantly, in the strategic arc stretching from Pakistan to Lebanon, there are as many Shias as there are Sunnis, and in the Persian Gulf region Shias clearly predominate.

Shias Excluded from Power Until Iraq War

However, despite this demographic weight, Shias have been by and large an invisible political force, excluded from power whether in the majority or minority. In the Middle East, the Sunnis had come to believe in their manifest destiny to rule. Iraq made Shia empowerment possible and, by the same token, challenged the Sunni conception of the sectarian balance of power in the region. The fury of the Sunni insurgency in Iraq, the cool reception for Iraq's new government in the Arab world, and the vehement anti-Shiism on display in the Arab street all reflect anger at the rise of the Shia.

Whereas Sunnis reacted angrily to regime change in Iraq, Shias were far more willing to give the United States the benefit of the doubt. In Iraq, following the lead of their most senior spiritual leader, the Grand Ayatollah Ali al-Sistani, Shias refrained from either resisting U.S. occupation or responding to the Sunni insurgency's provocations. Armed with religious decrees, Shias then joined the revamped security services and wholeheartedly participated in elections. Even conservative ayatollahs in Iran supported the elections, and Iran itself was the first of Iraq's neighbors to recognize the new Iraqi government and extend support to it. Elsewhere, Shias began to clamor for elections of their own, seeing promise in political reform and democracy. In Saudi Arabia, the voter turn-out rate in Shia regions was twice as high as the national average in the first elections in that country. In Lebanon and Bahrain, Shias called for "one man one vote," and even Iran—then led by a reformist president—offered broader cooperation with the United States. Iraq seemed to have provided the United States with an opening to build new ties with the other half of the Middle East's population. But that moment of opportunity passed, and by the end of 2006, Shia politics had adopted a different tenor.

It is now clear that the close relations the United States initially enjoyed with Shia parties and community leaders in Iraq gave way, by 2006, to greater confrontation, and that Shia politics slipped from the hand of moderate forces and became dominated by radical militias and politicians. Nor was the trend limited to Iraq. There was a palpable turn in Shia attitudes in the region. While it was U.S. arms that made the Shia revival possible, it is increasingly Iran and anti-American gun-toting militias that are setting the tone for relations with the Shia. Facing growing instability in the Middle East, the United States has no greater challenge than to understand this rising force, why it could be turning away from America, and how to stop that from happening.

The Legacy of 2006

The year 2006 was a fateful one for Shia politics. In Iraq, escalating sectarian conflict raised the stock of the radical cleric Muqtada al-Sadr, as his Mahdi Army militia spread its control over Baghdad and the Shia south. To the north, war with Israel emboldened Hezbollah [a militant Shia group] just as it divided Lebanon along sectarian lines between Shias on the one side and a coalition of Christians and Sunnis on the other. After reformists failed to build on an opening of relations with the United States over Afghanistan—an opening evident in the collaboration between the United States and Iran at the Bonn conference that decided the fate of post-Taliban Afghanistan—they lost the presidency to the hardliner Mahmoud Ahmadinejad. The new president quickly ratcheted up tensions with the United States. This, along with Iran's continued pursuit of its nuclear program, escalated tensions with the United States and raised the stakes for Washington in Iraq and Lebanon, where Shia forces rely on Iran for support.

There is a sectarian thread that runs through all these conflicts, separating Shias from Sunnis in Iraq, Shias from Sunnis and Christians in Lebanon, and Iran from its Sunni Arab neighbors who sympathize with Sunnis in Iraq and Lebanon.

The Making of Sectarianism

The sectarian force in Middle East politics began with the regime change in Iraq in 2003. A majority in Iraq, and suppressed by decades of Saddam's brutal dictatorship, the Shia were quick to take advantage of the U.S. coalition's invasion to lay claim to the country's future. They embraced the American promise of democracy as Grand Ayatollah al-Sistani ordered his followers to vote in Iraq's elections and join its new government. Millions of Shias showed up at ballot boxes to transform Iraq into the first Arab Shia state. That inspired Shias—but not so the Sunnis—to clamor for more rights and influence wherever they lived, challenging centuries-old political establishments that had kept them on the margins.

The change in Shia fortunes has met with Sunni resistance. In Iraq, an equally anti-American and anti-Shia insurgency quickly organized to plunge the country into violence and ensnare the United States in a stalemate. Car bombs targeted Shia markets, police recruits, mosques, and religious figures. The violence aimed at intimidating Shias who were seen as collaborating with the coalition. For two years Shias showed remarkable restraint—although there were sporadic retaliations—in the face of bloody provocations by the Sunni insurgency. But the ferocity of the attacks eventually took its toll—on both the United States and the increasingly frustrated Shias. In late 2005, once it became clear that elections were not going to end the insurgency, the United States turned to Sunni politicians who had boycotted the elections. The U.S. hope was that Sunni cooperation would weaken the insurgency. The new approach included more public criticism of Shia political leaders and the government, and greater attention to Shia militias.

The Shia did not take kindly to the new strategy and interpreted it as a sign of weakening American resolve caused by frustration at the ferocity of the insurgency and successful lobbying in Washington by Arab governments. Their anxiety turned into anger in February 2006 when a massive bomb destroyed the Golden Mosque in Samarrah, one of the holiest Shia shrines. Wary Shias balked at calls for restraint, which they saw as only emboldening the insurgency. Militias with vengeance on their minds stepped into the breach to promise protection to a community that was rapidly losing its trust in the political process and the United States. The war between the insurgency and the United States thus became the war between the insurgency, the United States, and Shia militias. The U.S. military found itself on the same side as Shia militias in the larger fight against the Sunni insurgency, but then confronted those militias as it tried to stop sectarian violence.

Washington pressed Shia leaders to rein in their militias, but to no avail. They saw the insurgency as the source of the violence and insisted the United States focus on disarming it. But U.S. attention was shifting to bringing security to Baghdad and hence away from the insurgency. Growing tensions eventually weakened moderate Shia voices as more and more Shias saw the U.S. engagement of Sunnis as a failure. The insurgency was stronger a year after Sunnis joined the political process—bombing Shia neighborhoods at will and accounting for 80 percent of U.S. casualties by the end of 2006. Turning Shia politics away from radicalism requires not just breaking the hold of Shia militias, but also rolling back the insurgency—the fear of which produces support for the militias. The challenge before the new U.S. strategy is to accomplish this exact task.

Beyond Iraq: The Revival's Implications

The sectarian conflict in Iraq has implications for the whole Middle East. Long before Americans recognized sectarianism as a problem, it was already shaping attitudes beyond Iraq's borders. Not long after Saddam fell from power, King Abdullah of Jordan warned of an emerging Shia crescent stretching from Beirut to Tehran. Shia power and Sunni reaction to it was on everyone's mind, and the fear was that it would seep into the soil in the region.

Iran sees itself as a great power, and it is pursuing the nuclear capability that would confirm this self-image.

That fear came true during the month-long war in Lebanon in the summer of 2006. The war turned Hezbollah and Iran into regional power brokers and sent jubilant Shias into the streets in Iraq, Bahrain, and Saudi Arabia. Unable to influence the course of events, Sunni powers Jordan, Saudi Arabia, and Egypt found themselves pushed to the sidelines. The war even caught Al-Qaeda off-guard as it watched Hezbollah steal some of its thunder. The reaction of Sunni rulers and radicals was swift: they denounced Hezbollah's campaign as an Iranian-sponsored Shia power grab. The war popularized Hezbollah on the Sunni Arab street, but that did not close the sectarian divide that the fighting had exposed, especially as cease-fire tensions in Lebanon escalated in the following months, raising the possibility of yet another sectarian conflict in the region.

The Lebanon war showed that Iraq has rewritten the rules in the Middle East, adding sectarian loyalties to the mix to decide where allegiances lie. For the United States the war was a low point. It undermined U.S. prestige across the region, and Washington lost much of the goodwill it had gained with the Shia following the Iraq war. Shia views of America hardened as Washington refused to push for a cease-fire while the war devastated Shia towns, villages, and neighborhoods.

For Washington, developments in Lebanon and Iraq are part of the larger challenge of dealing with Iran. Iran sees itself as a great power, and it is pursuing the nuclear capability that would confirm this self-image. Since 2003 it has shown a more confident but also more radical face. President Ahmadinejad appears to take seriously the old revolutionary goal of positioning Iran as the leading country of the entire Muslim world—an ambition that requires focusing on hostility to Israel and the West, which tends to bring Arabs and Iranians, Sunni and Shia, together rather than divide them even as it demands efforts to push traditional Arab Sunni allies of the West off to the sidelines. Ahmadinejad has increased tensions with the West with his brazen criticisms of the United States, tough talk on the nuclear issue, and virulent attacks on Israel. This has worried Washington, which sees Iran as a negative influence in Lebanon and Iraq, where it has accused Iran of supplying Shia militias with deadly weapons. Washington is not alone. Israel is nervous about Iran's nuclear intentions. Sunni Arab governments, too, fear that Iran will overshadow them regionally, and in the Persian Gulf, monarchies worry about the spread of an aggressive Iranian hegemony over their domains. The prospect of Tehran dictating security and oil policy and, most worrisome, intervening on behalf of local Shia populations, has Sunni rulers across the region pressing Washington to confront Iran.

The United States faces an increasingly fractious Middle East in the grip of old and new conflicts, . . . all connected to the broader Shia revival and the Sunni reaction to it.

The United States sees Iran through the prism of the impasse over its nuclear program; but Iran is important to a broader set of American concerns in the Middle East, from Iraq and Afghanistan, to the Arab-Israeli conflict, to oil prices.

Tehran benefited from America's toppling of the Taliban and Saddam regimes, which were significant barriers to Iranian ambition and influence. As the occupation of Iraq constrained American power and tarnished American prestige, Iran seized the opportunity to spread its wings. Rising Iranian clout has been entwined with the Shia revival that swept across the Middle East in the wake of the Iraq and Lebanon wars. The United States sees Iranian moral and material support for Iraq's Shia parties and militias as destabilizing, but can do little to stop it. However, it is not Iraq that has most vividly showcased Iran's regional reach and ambitions, but the summer war between Israel and Hezbollah. Having supported Hezbollah and supplied it with sophisticated weaponry, Iran not surprisingly basked in the glory at the expense of the Sunni regimes that had condemned the Shia movement. Iran's shadow continues to loom large over Lebanon as Hezbollah is tightening its grip on Lebanon and the specter of civil war has come back to haunt the country.

What Iran sowed in Lebanon, it expects to reap in Iraq. Washington is debating the merits of talking to Iran about Iraq at a time when Tehran has hinted that it holds most of the cards, suggesting that if the United States wants to deal with Iran—not only over Iraq but also over Lebanon, the Palestinian issue, or Afghanistan—it has to accept Tehran's terms for such an engagement. It was with a view to reverse this attitude that Washington escalated pressure on Iran in the first months of 2007, hoping to convince Tehran that there are limits to its influence and that it would likely face a high cost if it were to overreach.

The United States faces an increasingly fractious Middle East in the grip of old and new conflicts, each with its own issues and tempo, but all connected to the broader Shia revival and the Sunni reaction to it apparent in the sectarian conflict in Iraq. To get the Middle East right, Washington must understand this new force and how it is shaping the region. Only then will it be able to appropriately manage the multiple con-flicts that are unfolding in the region, the alignments that they will produce, and the impact that they will leave on U.S. inter-ests.

U.S. Actions in the Middle East Fuel the Conflict Between Islam and the West

The Economist

The Economist *is a British-owned weekly news and international affairs publication.*

Ever since the terrorist attacks of September 2001, [U.S. president] George Bush has been telling Osama bin Laden and his al-Qaeda terrorist network they will fail in one of their main aims: to trigger a broad global conflict between America and its allies, and Islam. The president has called Islam a peaceful religion, bringing "hope and comfort" to over a billion people. To judge by opinion polls, many Muslims around the world are unimpressed. To them, America's actions in the Middle East tell a different story about Mr Bush's attitude to their faith. And the president may not be right when he says that a broad clash of civilisations can be avoided. To anyone skimming the headlines in recent weeks, it seems as though believers in an imminent clash between Islam and the West have plenty of new evidence to support their case.

Examples of Political Islam

Iran—the country whose 1979 revolution put political Islam on the modern map—is cocking a snook at its western critics. Its president vows to destroy Israel, and its nuclear researchers have defied the world by going back to work. In its present mood, Iran shows little interest in seeking "rehabilitation" by addressing the long list of western complaints, which include sponsoring terror.

Meanwhile, the leaders of al-Qaeda appear on videotapes to tell their supporters that the war against "crusaders" and

"Forty Shades of Green—Political Islam," *The Economist (US)*, vol. 378, February 4, 2006, p. 23. Copyright 2006 Economist Newspaper Ltd. Republished with permission of Economist Newspaper, conveyed through Copyright Clearance Center, Inc.

Jews is very much alive. Mr bin Laden warns that deadly attacks on America are still being planned. His [then] deputy, Ayman al-Zawahiri, appeared on the screen ... to declare that he ... survived an American attempt on his life and that Allah, not Uncle Sam, would set the hour of his death.

At the same time, an Islamist movement that many western governments regard as terrorist and untouchable is savouring its stunning victory in the Palestinian elections. The Hamas triumph has brought delight to all its fellow members of the international fraternity known as the Muslim Brotherhood—from the refugee camps of Amman in Jordan, where sweets were eagerly handed out by local Brotherhood leaders, to their well-organised counterparts in the Islamic diaspora in Europe. Whatever Hamas now does, its success may be remembered as the biggest victory for political Islam since Iran's Ayatollah [Ruholla] Khomeini brought to the modern world the idea that Islam might be a formula for governance, law and spreading revolution.

[Al-Qaeda is] furious with Hamas for compromising with secular liberal ideas by taking part in multi-party elections.

Divisions in Political Islam

For all these reasons, outside observers might be forgiven for thinking that political Islam, in various violent forms, was on the march against the West. In fact, the Islamist movement, though it may look monolithic from afar, is highly quarrelsome and diverse, and in many ways its internal divisions are deepening.

By no means everybody in the Muslim world rejoiced at the Hamas victory. It was disturbing in at least two different quarters. One was the corridors of power in Arab states, such as Jordan and Egypt, where the Brotherhood is already a powerful grass-roots movement and is steadily gaining confidence. In Egypt's partially-free elections ... [in] November [2005], the Brotherhood did far better than expected; and in Jordan, where the Brothers have long been treated as an innocuous vent for letting off anti-Israel and anti-western steam, the movement is demanding a higher profile.

Even more dismayed by the Hamas victory, it seems, are the al-Qaeda terrorist network and its sympathisers. They were already furious with Hamas for compromising with secular liberal ideas by taking part in multi-party elections, and the fact that Hamas has played the democratic game rather successfully will only increase their dismay.

Here lies a paradox. The two best known forms of political Islam (broadly speaking, al-Qaeda and the Brotherhood) have common ideological origins. Both have their roots in the anti-secular opposition in Egypt, a conservative reading of Sunni Islam and the wealth and religious zeal of the Saudis. But they differ hugely over politics and tactics.

Tactical Allies, Doctrinal Enemies

The ideologists of al-Qaeda reject the division of the world into modern states. To them, the only boundaries that matter are between Islam (of which they believe they are the only authentic representatives) and infidels. By contrast, Hamas and Brotherhood thinking is pragmatic, accepting the reality of national boundaries.

Then compare political Islam among the Sunnis to the Shia variety, of which Iran is the vanguard. Vast religious differences, stemming from a split that occurred in the seventh century, separate these groups. They still give a sharp edge to the conflicts of the present day, most obviously in Iraq, where thousands of lives have been lost in Sunni-Shia violence.

In its doctrine and ethos, the simple, back-to-basics Sunni Islam from which the Brotherhood and al-Qaeda sprang is about as different as any Muslim practice could be from the sophisticated, scholarly world of the Iranian Shias, with their elaborate clerical hierarchy and long tradition of studying and adding to a corpus of texts. But when it comes to operational matters, especially against Israel, terrorist groups sponsored by Iran have no qualms about tactical co-operation with their Sunni counterparts. Hamas, for example, has good working relations with the al-Quds Force, an external arm of the Iranian Revolutionary Guard [part of Iran's military]. And suicide bombings against Israeli civilians, now regarded as a Hamas trademark, were probably inspired at first by Hezbollah, an Iranian-backed, Shia movement based in Lebanon.

Yet doctrinal differences matter . . . [and], there has been an escalation of the war of words between al-Qaeda supporters on one hand and Hamas and the Brotherhood on the other. In January [2006], a London-based website that reflects jihadist views—the belief in a broad, inexorable conflict between Islam and the West—cited 102 clerics, living and dead, to support the view that good Muslims should not take part in elections. For this ideological camp, any electoral exercise merely reinforces the blasphemous way of thinking that places human choices and regimes above the law of God. In the words of Stephen Ulph, an analyst of Islam at the Jamestown Foundation, a think-tank, al-Qaeda's message to Hamas is something like this: "You're still playing the western game—we can put away the chess board."

Practical Challenges for Political Islam

Now that Hamas faces the reality of power and day-to-day challenges of administration, it must decide how much more of a "western game" it is prepared to play. It has already watered down its Islamist fervour by entering policy debates with its secularist, Palestinian-nationalist rivals in the Fatah movement [a moderate Palestinian group] and may soon be deliberating the pros and cons of a tactical compromise with Israel.

And part of that dilemma will be ideological. Hamas leaders will need a theological licence from the Brotherhood's spiritual guides for the political choices they make. At the same time, the world Brotherhood has a huge stake in the success of a Hamas government which could be a model of political Islam. For exactly that reason, predicts Ziad Abu Amr, a Palestinian legislator close to Hamas, the Brotherhood is likely in the end to provide "doctrinal cover and political support" for whatever decisions Hamas takes. But if those decisions include compromise with Israel, the doctrinal bit will not be easy. Despite its rejection of violence in most circumstances, the Brotherhood's bottom lines have included deep ideological opposition to Israel's existence and a demand for Muslim control over Jerusalem.

Woe betide any western strategist who thinks the problems of the Muslim world can be addressed by a policy of "divide and rule".

Given that theology will play a role, at least, in these deliberations, it is worth studying the ways in which different Islamist movements converge and differ. Al-Qaeda and the Brotherhood, for example, are both loosely articulated international movements which claim to operate, often through proxies and ideological soul-mates, in scores of countries. Both have emerged out of the conservative wing of Sunni Islam, which believes in sticking to the letter of the earliest texts as the main form of spiritual guidance.

In other ways, al-Qaeda and the Brotherhood are entirely different phenomena. Al-Qaeda is first and foremost a movement which sponsors and co-ordinates acts of violence, not just in the Islamic heartland but anywhere it can hit back at the western enemy. In the ideology of the Brotherhood, including Hamas, resort[ing] to violence is justified only in the exceptional circumstances of "self-defence" and "occupation"—

conditions which are deemed to exist in Israel, the West Bank and American-occupied Iraq. . . .

Benefits for America?

Observing the ideological fights between al-Qaeda and the Brotherhood, and the physical fights between Sunnis and Shias [the two sects of Islam], some American strategists might ask themselves: since they all oppose us and our allies, shouldn't we take comfort from the fact that they hate each other too?

In reality, things don't work that way. However little the arcana of Sunni or Shia theology are understood in Peoria [a small city in Illinois] or even in Washington, DC, the hard fact is that the American occupation of Iraq has made it appear, to many people in the Middle East, that America is now the main arbiter in the balance of power between the different components of the Islamic world. To put it another way, people who were already inclined to see almost every development in the Islamic world as America's work will be harder to dissuade.

Despite the darkening clouds in America's relationship with Iran, many Sunni Muslims are convinced that the Bush administration is subverting their faith by favouring the Shia cause in Iraq and hence promoting Iranian influence. In the slums of eastern Amman, for example, people hardly knew what Shia Islam was until recently. Now the word has spread that neighbouring Iraq is about to get a Shia-dominated government—and, moreover, that it is all America's fault.

Nor can America escape this opprobrium by tilting its Iraqi policy a few degrees in a more pro-Sunni direction. Anything that seems to favour the Sunnis can also be interpreted as giving heart to the Saudi establishment, royal or clerical. And that in turn will be seen as a boost to Saudi efforts to spread various forms of Sunni fundamentalism all over the world.

The contrasts between different varieties of Islam, and Islamism, are not trivial—either in their teachings or the behaviour they inspire. The western world needs to know about them, if only to know which outcomes and shifts of policy are conceivable, and which are not. But woe betide any western strategist who thinks the problems of the Muslim world can be addressed by a policy of "divide and rule". The most likely result of that is that western countries will be blamed for divisions that have already existed, in one form or another, since the founding of Islam.

Current
CONTROVERSIES

CHAPTER 2

Should the United States Withdraw Its Troops from Iraq?

Chapter Preface

The 2003 U.S. invasion of Iraq was conducted in the wake of the September 11, 2001, terrorist attack on the United States—an attack carried out by al Qaeda, a radical Islamic terrorist group then based in Afghanistan. After the U.S. military ousted the group from Afghanistan along with the Taliban government that supported its terrorist activities, the United States turned its attention to Iraq. Although the Iraqi invasion was initially justified by U.S. policy makers as necessary to prevent Iraqi dictator Saddam Hussein from acquiring and using weapons of mass destruction (WMD), officials from the George W. Bush administration also frequently portrayed the Iraq war as part of a global war on terror aimed at eradicating the influence and strength of al Qaeda and its allies. This antiterrorist justification became especially important after no WMD were found in Iraq. Vice President Dick Cheney was the most vocal government official on this topic, claiming even as late as 2004 that Iraq had a relationship with al Qaeda.

Critics, however, pointed out that al Qaeda had no ties with Iraq prior to the American invasion, and the 9/11 Commission, an official entity set up by the U.S. government to investigate the 9/11 attack, agreed that there was "no collaborative relationship" between Iraq and al Qaeda before September 11, 2001. The administration, critics argued, falsely sought to link Iraq with al Qaeda and 9/11 to bolster public support for the war. The real plan, many commentators have concluded, was to establish American military bases in Iraq as part of a strategy to control the Middle East and ensure American access to its vast oil resources. Administration officials may have reasoned that Americans would not support the war if they believed it was being fought for oil.

The irony is that the Iraq war has now created an al Qaeda stronghold in Iraq that did not exist prior to the U.S. invasion. Even U.S. intelligence agents admit that the presence of large numbers of U.S. troops in Iraq was a massive recruitment opportunity for al Qaeda that boosted the group's ranks, drew supporters to Iraq, and allowed al Qaeda to grow into a global terrorist network. Today, al Qaeda fighters are a major part of an Iraqi insurgency that has disrupted U.S. plans to stabilize and reconstruct the country and cost the United States dearly—both in terms of American troop deaths and injuries and hundreds of billions of dollars in military war expenses. Although the number of al Qaeda insurgents in Iraq may only number a few thousand, American military officials in Iraq view them as a serious threat.

The first leader of al Qaeda fighters in Iraq was Abu Musab al-Zarqawi, until he was killed by U.S. troops in June 2006 and succeeded by Abu Hamza al-Muhaijir (also known as Abu Ayyub al-Masri). Under these leaders, al Qaeda insurgents in Iraq have conducted fatal suicide bomb attacks on U.S. troops, Iraqi government officials and police, and Iraqi civilians. Early in the war, al Qaeda joined forces with Iraqi Sunnis, members of the Sunni Islamic sect, a minority group that once governed Iraq. As a result, many of al Qaeda's attacks against civilians have targeted Shias, or Shi'ites, members of the Shia sect of Islam. Shias make up the majority of Iraq's population and have long been excluded from power but now dominate in Iraq's democratically elected government. Al Qaeda's strategy has been to incite sectarian violence between the Shias and the Sunnis, in order to draw the country into civil war. Al Qaeda's ultimate goals in Iraq appear to be to force U.S. troops to leave the country so al Qaeda can establish a fundamentalist Islamic government there. Bush administration officials now argue that U.S. troops must stay in Iraq in order to prevent al Qaeda from establishing a base there that they could use to attack Americans and their allies around the world.

Four years into the war, however, the U.S. military has yet to be able to crush the al Qaeda insurgency in Iraq. Numerous campaigns have been waged to root out this terrorist element, but although U.S. troops have been very efficient at clearing out insurgents from various towns or regions of Iraq, they have not established a permanent presence to hold these territories and prevent insurgents from returning. In 2007, however, the Bush administration named General David Petraeus to lead the American effort in Iraq and authorized a "surge" of approximately thirty thousand additional troops to the country. General Petraeus, who is considered an expert on counterinsurgency tactics, implemented a new strategy that emphasized stationing U.S. troops in Iraqi communities to prevent those locales from falling back into insurgents' control. This strategy is credited with stabilizing some parts of Baghdad, the capital of Iraq.

In addition, General Petraeus sought to form alliances with Iraqi tribal leaders to encourage them to oppose al Qaeda violence. This tactic appeared to be working, especially in Anbar province, a part of western Iraq considered to be the home of the Sunni insurgency. After tribal sheiks in Anbar began cooperating with U.S. forces, suicide attacks there dropped by 60 percent. In June 2007, General Petraeus made similar agreements with Iraqi tribes in the Baghdad area. The hope is that these alliances will force al Qaeda fighters out of Iraq. This result would satisfy the U.S. goal of keeping al Qaeda terrorists from forming a base in Iraq, but it may do little to quell the civil war between Iraqi Shias and Sunnis.

Whether General Petraeus will have enough time to accomplish the goal of ridding Iraq of al Qaeda, however, may depend on how much longer U.S. troops stay in the country. The continuing Iraq war is seen by many people at home as a huge policy failure and it has become a hotly debated political issue within the United States. The following viewpoints address this issue and present a sampling of opinions on the important question of whether and when U.S. troops should be withdrawn from Iraq.

The Iraq War Has Failed

Ibrahim M. Oweiss

Ibrahim M. Oweiss is a professor at the Georgetown University School of Foreign Service in Qatar.

On Jan. 4, 2007, Sen. Joseph R. Biden, Jr. (D-DE), chairman of the Senate Foreign Relations Committee, said he believes "top officials in the [George W.] Bush administration have privately concluded they have lost Iraq and are simply trying to postpone disaster so the next president will be the guy landing helicopters inside the Green Zone, taking people off the roof in a chaotic withdrawal reminiscent of Vietnam."

It has become evident in the United States and elsewhere in the world that the U.S. has failed in its war on Iraq and seems to have no easy way out. Attacks on the current Bush administration are mounting, from Democrats and Republicans alike. American public opinion, as evidenced by the low approval rating of President George W. Bush, reflects dissatisfaction and dismay over the Iraq war. It is a war that has lasted longer than the U.S. involvement in World War II and resulted in more than 3,000 American soldiers killed, tens of thousands injured, and hundreds of thousands of Iraqi civilians dead and injured—in addition to the cost of destruction in Iraq on the one hand and, on the other, the negative consequences of the war on the U.S. economy. Indeed, this war has contributed to the largest budget deficit and national debt in U.S. history.

Reasons Behind the Failure

The first reason for the U.S. failure in Iraq is the current administration's dependence on a military option. Less than three months after the U.S. invasion, former President Bill

Ibrahim M. Oweiss, "Why Did the United States Fail in Its War on Iraq?" *Washington Report on Middle East Affairs*, vol. 26, May–June 2007, pp. 34–36. Copyright 2007 American Educational Trust. All rights reserved. Reproduced by permission.

Clinton told me in a June 16, 2003 interview at his New York City office, "I wish this administration understood the limitations of the military option." With the world's strongest military, the Bush administration thought it could win any war, a matter which is not in dispute. Winning a military victory, however, is not sufficient. More important is to win peace in the aftermath.

The Bush administration repeatedly claimed that Saddam Hussein was lying when he stated that Iraq had no WMD . . . [but] he was not.

The second reason was the haste in rushing to war on Iraq on March 19, 2003. Given sufficient time, the United Nations may have been able to prove that Iraq did not have weapons of mass destruction, and thus remove the rationale for war. Instead, the administration's rush to war meant it did not have enough time for thorough military planning. The decision to wage war on Iraq was based mainly on advice from Pentagon "civilians" with no background in military combat, such as Paul Wolfowitz, Douglas Feith and Richard Perle. The military apparatus was not given sufficient time to adequately prepare for the war or suggest the need for a more sizeable military deployment. Moreover—and more crucially—there was no clear blueprint for a post-war plan of action.

The third reason for the U.S. failure is that the war on Iraq was internationally illegal, as stated by former U.N. Secretary-General Kofi Annan. Not only does it represent a violation of international law—because it was conducted against a sovereign state and a full member of the United Nations that represented no threat to the United States and had no links with al-Qaeda—but it also sets a serious precedent in recent world affairs in its undermining of the United Nations.

Domestically, however, the war was not unconstitutional once Congress voted to authorize it. Yet it is this vote that leads to the fourth reason for the U.S. failure—the claim that Iraq possessed weapons of mass destruction (WMD). The Bush administration, along with British Prime Minister Tony Blair, insisted that Iraq had WMD, and sold the idea to the American people and Congress, even showing pictures of such weapons on television. The hard sell helped the Bush administration gain congressional approval even before the U.N. had completed its full investigation. The Bush administration repeatedly claimed that Saddam Hussein was lying when he stated that Iraq had no WMD. As it turned out, however, he was not. History will therefore be the judge as to who was the liar.

Changing Rationales for War

In an embargoed interview with *The Washington Post*'s Bob Woodward in 2004 released only after his death, former President Gerald Ford expressed strong disagreement with the rationale for the war on Iraq. He said he would have pushed alternatives, such as sanctions, much more vigorously. A little more than a year after the invasion Ford told Woodward, "I don't think I would have gone to war."

In the tape-recorded interview, Ford was critical not only of Bush but also of Vice President Dick Cheney—chief of staff for the late president—as well as then-Defense Secretary Donald H. Rumsfeld, who also served as Ford's chief of staff, and then his secretary of defense.

> *World-renowned thinker Noam Chomsky made a persuasive argument for the true reason behind the invasion of Iraq. That reason ... is oil.*

"Rumsfeld and Cheney and the president made a big mistake in justifying going into the war in Iraq. They put the emphasis on weapons of mass destruction," Ford said. "And now, I've never publicly said I thought they made a mistake, but I felt very strongly it was an error in how they should justify what they were going to do."

On the same point, Sen. Gordon H. Smith (R-OR), who originally had voted for the war, said on Dec. 7, 2006, "I for one, am at the end of my rope when it comes to supporting a policy that has our soldiers patrolling the same streets in the same way, being blown up by the same bombs day after day. . . . That is absurd. It may even be criminal."

Acknowledging that he had been "rather silent" on Iraq following his 2002 vote in support of the war, Smith said, "I cannot tell you how devastated I was to learn that in fact we were not going to find weapons of mass destruction." The Oregon senator now represents the views of "moderate" Republicans.

It was only after the war on Iraq had been launched that the administration, now doubtful of finding WMD, resorted to another rationale and adopted the rhetoric of "democratizing" the Middle East as an integral part of the overall war against terrorism. Of course, the link between democracy and terrorism defies logic. The IRA [Irish Republican Army] was a terrorist organization in the heart of a democratic society. A terrorist attack was carried out on a Japanese subway.

While democracy certainly is a laudable goal, history shows that it cannot be imposed from the outside. In order to be self-sustained, democracy must be home grown. Instead, however, as E.J. Dionne Jr. wrote in the Dec. 8, 2006 *Washington Post*, "One of the many disastrous consequences of President Bush's botched policy in Iraq is that it has given the promotion of democracy a bad name. In truth," Dionne went on to say, "this Middle East adventure was never a serious effort to build democracy in Saddam Hussein's Iraq. Yes, there were elections and there was a lot of talk about democracy. But don't listen to what the administration said. Look at what it did. This war has done enormous damage to the United States, and some of the damage is to our ideals. An administration that fought a misguided, poorly planned and ill-considered war in the name of democracy should not be allowed to discredit the democratic idea itself," he concluded.

In a Dec. 27, 2006 interview, world-renowned thinker Noam Chomsky made a persuasive argument for the true reason behind the invasion of Iraq. That reason, Chomsky argued, is oil. The fifth reason for the failure of the U.S. war on Iraq, then, was the lack of vision of the invasion's true goals. Certainly the changing rationale for the war must have had a psychological effect on the U.S. soldiers sent to the inferno of war.

On Jan. 5, 2007, President Bush met with 13 senators at the White House opposed to his plans to send more troops to Iraq, as reported by Sheryl Gay Stolberg in the Jan. 8 *International Herald Tribune*. After the meeting Sen. Larry Craig (R-ID) said that Bush "got an earful, and I think appropriately so." Sen. Barack Obama (D-IL) told the president that sending more troops to-Iraq "was a mistake," and Sen. Arlen Specter (R-PA) said he, too, was opposed. Sen. Mary Landrieu (D-LA) complained of having "a much harder time convincing my constituents that a victory is achievable."

The above are some of the reasons why our war on Iraq not only has failed but has ignited sectarianism, massive daily killings and de facto civil war.

The Iraq War Has Increased the Threat of Terrorism

Jean-Louis Bruguiere

Jean-Louis Bruguiere is the first vice president of the Tribunal de Grande Instance (Court of Great Claim) in Paris and responsible for all terrorism-related matters in the Middle East as they apply to France.

No one can deny that today's terrorist threat is particularly high. It reached an extremely dangerous level at the dawn of 2007. . . . The terrorist threat has grown continuously and diversified itself by constantly multiplying its networks on a global scale. Now, for the first time in history, no region of the world is safe. . . .

Terror Diversified

The Islamic threat not only has become globalized, it has developed a globalized strategy of attack. This can be seen in terms of targets and the means used. In 2001, Al Qaeda and the other terrorist networks that had joined them—or that share the same ideology—shifted from traditional methods of bombing to using civilian aircraft as weapons of mass destruction. These have been developed through diversification, with the sole objective of intensifying the message of terror.

Suicide bombing operations used by Palestinian organizations and Chechen terrorists now are, since the Iraqi conflict, also employed by the terrorist networks that have joined the movement of the late Abu Musab al-Zarqawi [Al Qaeda's leader in Iraq]. This diversification of methods also is illustrated by the capacity of certain networks to use unconven-

Jean-Louis Bruguiere, "On the Defensive: 'One Thing Is Certain. . . . Military Intervention in Iraq and the Climate of Open Rebellion That Ensued Profoundly Have Altered the Terms of the [Terrorist] Threat and Now Condition Its Development.'" *USA Today Magazine*, May 2007, Vol. 135, Iss. 2744, p. 28.

tional weapons—chemical, biological, or even radioactive—known as "dirty bombs." These are not merely suppositions, but serious hypotheses that must be considered by the Western intelligence and anti-terrorist services.

In 2002, France successfully dismantled a radical Islamic network that intended to attack its territory using toxic substances. Europe incontestably has become a major target for Al Qaeda since the strengthening of the role of the GSPC [an Algerian Islamic terrorist group]. Yet, it is not the sole target, either geographically or in terms of the terrorists' motives and objectives. Al Qaeda and the organizations and structures working alongside it adeptly have integrated methods of communication into their strategy by using satellite television channels and the Internet. This opportunistic use of media broadcasting, digital transmission, and provocation to communicate threats has become Al Qaeda's new weapon, helping them promote their specific objectives as well as the general feeling of insecurity and fear. Besides mastering the use of these Al Qaeda has the details of the global economy into its strategy, particularly the interdependence of financial markets and their volatility, the energy crisis, and commodities exchanges.

In the face of this global [terrorist] threat, the reaction of the democratic, especially Western, countries . . . is fragile and lacks unity.

International terrorism of Islamic origin, which is characterized as being all at once highly decentralized, polymorphous in its structures and organization, everchanging, and global, is at the center of the problems and risks that our societies are facing. These risks threaten our collective safety and the individual liberties that are the basis of our democratic societies. They likewise are political and geopolitical, as shown by the Iraqi dilemma and recent developments in the Middle

East. Finally, the risks are societal and environmental, and could lead to economic or monetary crises through terrorist action.

A Fragile West

In the face of this global threat, the reaction of the democratic, especially Western, countries and the regimes associated with them is fragile and lacks unity. As yet, we have been unable to agree upon a global and unified anti-terrorist approach, given that we have not even managed to agree upon a common definition of terrorism. Despite the gravity of the situation, it seems that a certain egocentrism reigns and that the individual interests of states prevail. The European Union—with its 450,000,000 consumers—is a major player in the global economy, despite its political disparities and the absence of a constitution that would legitimize its institutions. In the past decade, Europe especially has seen the growth of militant Islamic networks and groups devoted to the Salafist [GSPC] cause, which today have joined the elusive Al Qaeda movement. This radical Islamic movement based in Europe has profited from these disparities and from the resulting legal and institutional loopholes that have prevented the implementation of a united and consistent European terrorist prevention policy, even if significant progress has been made in this field. So far, Europe has encountered real difficulties in efficiently managing the double-edged problem of immigration and integration of the immigrant population into our societies. . . .

The post-Communist era led to a divided and antagonistic world in which nationalist tensions and radical ideologies were exacerbated.

The terrorist threat feeds on various rapidly changing opportunistic factors, which are extremely hard to quantify or analyze. These mainly are ideological and political, but are social, economic, and even existential in nature as well. Moreover, regional conflicts, political crises, and extremely sensitive geographical zones exacerbate the intensity of the threat, which unquestionably is on the rise—and its progression in the short and medium term does not give any cause for optimism. In France, the threat level currently is four on a scale of one to five.

Terrorism Was Predictable

Yet, is the rise of terrorism inevitable, and could this development have been predicted? The origins of the tragic events of 9/11 certainly were detectable. They should have been anticipated during the decade leading up to them. The Sept. 11 attacks were not an accident of history or a terrible stroke of fate. They took seed in a gradual change born of a long-standing division. After the fall of communism, the West dreamt of a new world that would enjoy an era of prosperity and freedom, but this was forgetting other realities. The post-Communist era led to a divided and antagonistic world in which nationalist tensions and radical ideologies were exacerbated. Some of them, cultivating hatred, took on a theological label. . . .

All the Western countries demonstrated a terrible naivete and negligence in the face of this irrepressible rise in terrorist violence. This development should have been anticipated; even at that time, the anti-terrorist experts should have been able to see it coming. It took the tragic events of Sept. 11, 2001, for the U.S. and the rest of the world to wake up to the extent of the horrific reality of the terrorist threat. A radical, global, violent, and dedicated terrorism was spurred on by Al Qaeda and supported by countless networks and activist cells sharing the same strategy. These networks have developed rapidly and are spreading all over the world, with no centralized command structure.

Islamic terrorism is a response to economic globalization, but also the spread of democratic ideals. These developments irrevocably condemned all sectarian and repressive ideologies and totalitarian regimes. For Al Qaeda, the only response was to use violence and spread fear. Therefore, once the split between communism and capitalism was no more, the radical Islamic movement would base its strategy of reprisal on promoting a violent jihad throughout the world. It is clear that this threat has diversified and spread around the globe over the years. This threat is highly splintered, profoundly evolving, and spreading like a tumor. Despite the archaic ideology underlying the radical Islamic movement, it has a growing capacity to use cutting edge technology. These attributes provide a measure of the difficulty of the task ahead of us.

Iraq Fans the Flames

The current level of the threat largely is due to the situation in Iraq. If the military reaction of the U.S. and its allies in Afghanistan after 9/11 put Al Qaeda on the defensive, the Iraqi issue gave it a new impetus. Europe became a priority flash point, but other regions of the world also have been targeted, especially Southeast Asia. At the same time, the jihad sympathizers have become even more radical and have diversified their strategies in terms of targets and methods. From 2001–03, Al Qaeda and its supporters, through isolated but highly symbolic operations—the bombing of a synagogue in Djerba [Tunisia], attempting to sink a petrol tanker in Yemen, and the attacks in Karach [Pakistan]—are a means of showing the world that they remain very capable of taking action.

At the same time, another epicenter has replaced Afghanistan: Chechnya and the Caucasus region. . . . Thus, neither the collapse of the Taliban regime, nor the capture or neutralization of the leaders of Al Qaeda, nor even the anti-terrorist procedures set in motion all around the world have been able to curb this threat.

The Costs of the Iraq War Are Astronomical

Andrew Stephen

Andrew Stephen is U.S. editor of the British news magazine the New Statesman.

They roar in every day, usually direct from the Landstuhl US air-force base in the Rhineland [Western Germany] giant C-17 cargo planes capable of lifting and flying the 65-tonne M1 Abrams tank to battlefields anywhere in the world. But Landstuhl is the first staging post for transporting most of the American wounded in Iraq and Afghanistan back to the United States, and these planes act as CCATs ("critical care air transport") with their AETs—"aeromedical evacuation teams" of doctors, nurses and medical technicians, whose task is to make sure that gravely wounded US troops arrive alive and fit enough for intensive treatment at the Walter Reed Army Medical Centre . . . in Washington.

These days it is de rigueur [obligatory] for all politicians, ranging from President [George W.] Bush and Ibrahim al-Jaafari (Iraq's "prime minister") to junior congressmen, to visit the 113-acre Walter Reed complex to pay tribute to the valour of horribly wounded soldiers. Last Christmas [2006], the centre was so overwhelmed by the 500,000 cards and presents it received for wounded soldiers that it announced it could accept no more.

The Costs of American Wounded

Yet the story of the US wounded reveals yet another deception by the Bush administration, masking monumental miscalculations that will haunt generations to come. Thanks to the work

Andrew Stephen, "Iraq: The Hidden Cost of the War; America Won't Simply Be Paying with its Dead. The Pentagon Is Trying to Silence Economists Who Predict that Several Decades of Care for the Wounded Will Amount to an Unbelievable $2.5 Trillion," *New Statesman*, vol. 136, March 12, 2007, pp. 26–29. Copyright © 2007 New Statesman, Ltd. Reproduced by permission.

of a Harvard professor and former Clinton administration economist named Linda Bilmes, and some other hardworking academics, we have discovered that the administration has been putting out two entirely separate and conflicting sets of numbers of those wounded in the wars.

This might sound like chicanery by George W Bush and his cronies—or characteristic incompetence—but Bilmes and Professor Joseph Stiglitz, the Nobel laureate economist from Columbia University, have established not only that the number wounded in Iraq and Afghanistan is far higher than the Pentagon has been saying, but that looking after them alone could cost present and future US taxpayers a sum they estimate to be $536bn [billion], but which could get considerably bigger still. Just one soldier out of the 1.4 million troops so far deployed who has returned with a debilitating brain injury, for example, may need round-the-clock care for five, six, or even seven decades. In present-day money, according to one study, care for that soldier alone will cost a minimum of $4.3m [million].

Miscalculation of War Costs

However, let us first backtrack to 2002–2003 to try to establish why the administration's sums were so wildly off-target. Documents just obtained under the Freedom of Information Act show how completely lost the Bush administration was in Neverland when it came to Iraq: Centcom, the main top-secret military planning unit at [former U.S. secretary of defense] Donald Rumsfeld's Pentagon, predicted in its war plan that only 5,000 US troops would be required in Iraq by the end of 2006.

Rummy's [former] deputy Paul Wolfowitz was such a whizz at the economics of it all that he confidently told us that Iraq would "really finance its own reconstruction". Rumsfeld himself reported that the administration had come up with "a number that's something under $50bn" as the cost of the war. Larry Lindsey, then assistant to the president on economic policy at the White House, warned that it might actually soar to as much as $200bn—with the result that Bush did as he habitually does with those who do not produce convenient facts and figures to back up his fantasies: he sacked him.

From official statistics supplied by the non-partisan Congressional Budget Office, we now know that the Iraq war is costing roughly $200m a day, or $6bn every month; the total bill so far is $400bn. But, in their studies, Bilmes and Stiglitz consider three scenarios that were not even conceivable to Bush, Rummy, Wolfowitz et al back in 2003. In the first, incurring the lowest future costs, troops will start to be withdrawn [in 2007] and be out by 2010. The second assumes that there will be a gradual withdrawal that will be complete by 2015. The third envisages the participation of two million servicemen and women, with the war going on past 2016.

Estimating long-term costs using even the second, moderate scenario, Bilmes tells me: "I think we are now approaching a figure of $2.5 trillion." This, she says, "includes three kinds of costs. It includes the cash costs of running the combat operations, the long-term costs of replenishing military equipment and taking care of the veterans, and [increased costs] at the Pentagon. And then it includes the economic cost, which is the differential between reservists' pay in their civilian jobs and what they're paid in the military—and the macroeconomic costs, such as the percentage of the oil-price increase."

Let me pause to explain those deceptive figures. Look at the latest official toll of US fatalities and wounded in the media, and you will see something like 3,160 dead and 23,785 wounded. . . . From this, you might assume that only 11,000 or so troops, in effect, have been wounded in Iraq. But Bilmes discovered that the Bush administration was keeping two separate sets of statistics of those wounded: one issued by the Pentagon and therefore used by the media, and the other by the Department of Veterans Affairs [VA]—a government department autonomous from the Pentagon. At the beginning of [2007], the Pentagon was putting out a figure of roughly 23,000 wounded, but the VA was quietly saying that more than 50,000 had, in fact, been wounded.

Long-term costs [of the Iraq war] . . . 'are now approaching a figure of $2.5 trillion.'

Casualty Conspiracy

To draw attention to her academic findings, Bilmes wrote a piece for the *Los Angeles Times* of 5 January 2007 in which she quoted the figure of "more than 50,000 wounded Iraq war soldiers". The reaction from the Pentagon was fury. An assistant secretary there named Dr William Winkenwerder phoned her personally to complain. Bilmes recalls: "He said, 'Where did you get those numbers from?'" She explained to Winkenwerder that the 50,000 figure came from the VA and faxed him copies of official US government documents that proved her point. Winkenwerder backed down.

Matters did not rest there. Despite its independence from the Pentagon, the VA is run by Robert James Nicholson, a former Republican Party chairman and Bush's loyal political appointee. Following Bilmes's exchange with Winkenwerder—on 10 January [2007], to be precise—number of wounded listed on the VA website dropped from 50,508 to 21,649. The Bush administration had, once again, turned reality on its head to concur with its claims. "The whole thing is scary," Bilmes says. "I have never been conspiracy-minded, but watching them change the numbers on the website—it's extraordinary."

What Bilmes had discovered was that the tally of US fatalities in Iraq and Afghanistan included the outcome of "nonhostile actions", most commonly vehicle accidents. But the Pentagon's statistics of the wounded did not. Even troops incapacitated for life in Iraq or Afghanistan—but not in "hostile situations"—were not being counted, although they will require exactly the same kind of medical care back home as soldiers similarly wounded in battle. Bilmes and Stiglitz had set out, meantime, to explore the ratio of wounded to deaths in previous American wars. They found that in the First World War, on average 1.8 were wounded for every fatality; in the Second World War, 1.6; in Korea, 2.8; in Vietnam, 2.6; and, in the first Gulf war in 1991, 1.2. In this war, 21st-century medical care and better armour have inflated the numbers of the wounded-but-living, leading Bilmes to an astounding conclusion: for every soldier dying in Iraq or Afghanistan today, 16 are being wounded. The Pentagon insists the figure is nearer nine—but, either way, the economic implications for the future are phenomenal.

[The Veterans Administration] is quite unable to cope with a workload that the Bush administration did not foresee.

So far, more than 200,000 veterans from the current Iraq or Afghanistan wars have been treated at VA centres. Twenty per cent of those brought home are suffering from serious brain or spinal injuries, or the severing of more than one limb, and a further 20 per cent from amputations, blindness or deafness, severe burns, or other dire conditions. "Every person injured on active duty is going to be a long-term cost of the war," says Bilmes. If we compare the financial ramifications of the first Gulf war to the present one, the implications become even more stark. Despite its brevity, even the 1991 Gulf war exacted a heavy toll: 48.4 per cent of veterans sought medical care, and 44 per cent filed disability claims. Eighty-eight per cent of these claims were granted, meaning that 611,729 veterans from the first Gulf war are now receiving disability benefits; a large proportion are suffering from psychiatric illnesses, including post-traumatic stress disorder and depression.

More than a third of those returning from the current wars, too, have already been diagnosed as suffering from similar conditions. But although the VA has 207 walk-in "vet centres" and other clinics and offices throughout the US, it is a bureaucracy under siege. It has a well-deserved reputation for providing excellent healthcare for America's 24 million veterans, but is quite unable to cope with a workload that the Bush administration did not foresee.

Poor Care for Vets

There is now a backlog of 400,000 claims from veterans and waiting lists of months, some of which render . . . care virtually inaccessible, in the words of Frances Murphy, the VA's own deputy under-secretary for health. Claims are expected to hit 874,000 [in 2007], 930,000 in 2008. Casualties returning from Iraq meanwhile outnumber other patients at Walter Reed 17 to one, and many have to be put up at nearby hotels and motels rather than in the hospital beds they desperately need. Suicide attempts are frequent; often the less wounded end up having to care for the more seriously wounded.

Since I researched this piece, the *Washington Post* has published a series of articles outlining the chaos at Walter Reed and elsewhere. Undercover reporters found soldiers suffering from schizophrenia, post-traumatic stress and other brain injuries, occupying rooms infested with mice and cockroaches. The ensuing furor resulted in the sacking of the general in charge. Even Bush says he is "deeply troubled" by these "unacceptable" conditions at Walter Reed, but his government has carefully avoided the issue of how much it will cost to put right these wrongs. The failure to look after returning, often traumatised troops leads to yet further hidden costs to the US economy: the consequences of unemployment, family violence, crime, alcoholism and drug abuse, for example. . . .

A Legacy of Debt

It is sobering to think how the money going down the drain in Iraq could otherwise have been spent. "For this amount of money, we could have provided health insurance for the uninsured of this country," Bilmes tells me. "We could have made social security solvent for the next three generations, and implemented all the 9/11 Commission's recommendations [to tighten domestic security]."

That kind of list goes on: the annual cost of treating all heart disease and diabetes in the United States would amount to a quarter of what the Iraq war is costing. Pre-school for every child in America would take just $35bn, a year. In their main paper, Bilmes and Stiglitz come up with an even more intriguing possibility: "We could have had a Marshall Plan for the Middle East, or the developing countries, that might have succeeded in winning hearts and minds."

What a historic triumph that would have been for Bush. Instead, his legacy to generations of Americans will be a needless debt of at least $2.5trn [trillion], what his own defence secretary describes as a four-way civil war in Iraq, dangerous instability in the Middle East, and increasingly entrenched hatred of the United States throughout the world.

The Iraq War Does Not Improve U.S. Energy Security

Jerry Landay

Jerry Landay is a retired CBS News correspondent living in Bristol, Rhode Island, who writes on current issues.

After World War II, the president's national security council propounded a policy that would shape the world's geopolitical future: "Oil operations are, for all practical purposes, instruments of our foreign policy." More than a half-century later, that policy has not changed. With the invasion of Iraq already secretly being planned, freshly selected President George W. Bush listed "energy security" as his first action priority.

Energy security is the invisible elephant in Washington, guiding Bush policy on Iraq, the Middle East, Latin America, and Africa. It explains the "surge [in troop strength in Iraq]," the absence of an exit strategy from Iraq, the stubborn resistance of the Bush-Cheney team to efforts by the Congressional Democrats to impose a withdrawal deadline for 170,000 American soldiers, as well as the ongoing construction of permanent military bases in Iraq, and the costly stationing of thousands of American troops on foreign soil from Kuwait to Djibouti.

Energy security is the invisible presence shaping what the 2008 presidential candidates say or don't say about oil and energy. Energy security is the reason [presidential contender] Hillary Clinton refuses to embrace a withdrawal deadline and why Republican presidential hopeful John McCain declares that there is "no alternative Plan B" to the ongoing build-up of American forces.

Jerry Landay, "Iraq War Is All About Controlling the Oil," *The Providence Journal*, May 11, 2007. Copyright © 2007 The Providence Journal. Reproduced by permission.

In short, the American occupation and the maintenance of a shaky Iraqi government are the insurance policy for American control and access to the second largest untapped reserve of petroleum in the world. The politicians don't say much about an energy-security policy based on foreign oil. The news media don't report very much on it.

Oil Companies to Benefit from New Iraqi Law

The Big Five oil companies don't proclaim it in their self-promoting institutional advertising campaigns. Yet the so-called "Majors"—U.S.-based Exxon-Mobil, Chevron, and ConocoPhillips; the Dutch Shell Oil; and the British-owned British Petroleum—would be the principal beneficiaries of a new hydrocarbon law before the Iraqi Parliament that the press rarely mentions.

Waging costly resource wars ... in an age of terrorism only makes permanent the threat to American "energy security."

The initial draft, shaped by American contractors to the Iraqi government, has been amended by the U.S. Embassy in Iraq, and approved by the Iraqi Cabinet. The draft now awaits final approval by the Iraqi Parliament, but there is much reported Iraqi resistance to it, with good reason.

Oil Change International, an energy watchdog group, has devotedly tracked the proposed law. The law would reverse a trend in which most major petro-nations have largely nationalized their oil fields and reserves. Under the proposed Iraqi law, concessions involving 63 Iraqi oilfields, both developed and undeveloped, would go to major foreign-oil companies, assuring them of dominance over Iraqi oil for a generation or more. Only 17 already-developed fields would be directly controlled by a proposed Iraqi National Oil Company (INOC). . . .

The draft law grants assurance of "reasonable incentives" to foreign investors—the provision that kicks the door open to foreign developers. Development licenses are to be granted "on a competitive basis," a nod to outside companies with sufficient development capital.

Oil Change International states: "The law is a dramatic break from the past. Foreign oil companies will have a stake in Iraq's vast oil wealth for the first time since 1972, when Iraq nationalized the oil industry. This law would essentially open two-thirds of known—and all of [Iraq's] as yet undiscovered—reserves open to foreign control." According to Oil Change International, this amounts to 115 billion barrels of known oil reserves—10 percent of the world total.

The language of Article 11 of the draft law pays vague lip service to the principle of equal revenue sharing from petroleum and natural gas proceeds among . . . the Shi'as, Sunnis, and Kurds—supporting "distribution of . . . federal revenue allocation." But ConocoPhillips and Shell are already negotiating separate concessions with Kurdistan alone, and others reportedly will follow suit.

Oil Change International reports that foreign oil companies "would not have to invest their earnings in the Iraqi economy, partner with Iraqi companies, hire Iraqi workers or share new technologies. They could even ride out Iraq's current instability by signing contracts now, while the Iraqi government is at its weakest, and then wait at least two years before setting foot in the country."

The Path to Long-Term U.S. Security

Washington politicians understandably want to hedge the nation against the devastating impact on American life and the economy of a severe interruption of overseas oil supplies. But waging costly resource wars or granting discriminatory privileges to private interests that harm host oil states in an age of terrorism only makes permanent the threat to American "energy security."

Only "soft power"—peacemaking, smart diplomacy, constructive nation-building, generous sharing formulas, vigorous energy conservation and research policies at home—can assure long-term security for American interests without creating grievous new problems. It's time for leadership from politicians to acknowledge the existence of the elephant in the room and do something creative about it.

Permanent U.S. Bases in Iraq Will Only Worsen the Terrorist Threat

Thomas Gale Moore

Thomas Gale Moore is an economist and a senior fellow at the Hoover Institution, a public policy research group at Stanford University that focuses on politics and economic issues.

While the White House has often denied having a Plan B for Iraq, it turns out that the Pentagon has thought about what to do if Plan A, the "surge" doesn't work. According to Steve Inskeep and Guy Raz of National Public Radio, Plan B would involve maintaining a series of military bases around Iraq with some 30,000 to 40,000 U.S. troops. That plan would have them stay for decades, under the excuse that they could train the Iraqi troops and deter neighboring countries, such as Iran and Turkey, from sending their own troops into the country. Already the U.S. has built military compounds that look permanent, supplied with air-conditioning, movie theaters, Starbucks coffee houses, and fast food outlets.

An Old Idea

The idea is hardly new. For the last decade, the neocons have advocated that the U.S. establish bases in Iraq to police the Middle East and make the area safe for Israel. Although no one is totally certain why the Bush Administration took us into the quagmire of Iraq, it seems plausible that securing bases in that part of the world was one significant factor. At the time, the U.S. had major military installations in Saudi Arabia; but they had generated considerable opposition among the Saudis and in the rest of the Arab world, with the result that the Royal family was increasingly desirous of getting rid of them.

In 1998, [al Qaeda terrorist leader] Osama Bin Laden issued a Fatwa [proclamation] urging Jihad [religious war] Against Americans, ostensibly because American troops were now stationed on "sacred" soil, the land that contains Mecca and Medina. In the latest Republican debate, [presidential candidate Rep.] Ron Paul raised that issue, only to be widely criticized by the Republican right. Paul, however, was correct: that was a major factor in 9/11. The U.S. strong bias favoring Israel no doubt contributed as well. The twin towers were not brought down, however, because we attempted to provide equal rights for people of all genders or that we wear immodest clothing and live "immoral" lives. They were destroyed because of our foreign policy, in particular, because we had troops in Muslim parts of the world. We now have even more of them and are seen as a new version of the Crusades.

More Terrorism

This implies that, if we maintain a strong military presence in Muslim countries, including Iraq, we will continue to generate hatred and terrorism. Osama and his allies will persist in attacking us. Permanent or long term bases in Iraq will only bring more fire and brimstone to the world. The only way to reduce terrorism significantly is to leave the Middle East to the Middle Easterners.

The only way to prevent another 9/11 is to vacate the Middle East.

Why are we building the largest embassy in the world in Baghdad? Iraq is a relatively small, unimportant, and backward country sitting on a lot of oil. That the U.S is constructing this mammoth compound tells the world that it is planning to occupy that part of the globe for a long time. Iraq will become an unofficial colony used to police the rest of the Middle East.

In particular, the U.S. will be watching over Persia or, as it is now called, Iran. The Persians have a long and great history and will not relish the idea that a western Christian newcomer will be supervising their behavior. Nor will the Sunni [one sect of Islam] governments in the region look with favor on this "crusading" state's attempting to dictate their actions.

Bring U.S. Troops Home

The only way to prevent another 9/11 is to vacate the Middle East. We have no need to be there. Some would argue that our dependence on foreign oil requires that we control the largest supply of petroleum in the world. This is untrue; there is no necessity for America to rule the oil-rich territories. Countries with large supplies of oil have no use for that fuel except to sell it. All of those oil-based states have become dependent on the revenues that come from selling it. They have no choice. Nothing can be done with that liquid except market it. Even if radical Islamists take control of one of the petro-states, its government will still have to sell the oil to generate the revenue necessary to maintain its power.

Unfortunately, none of the presidential candidates, with the exception of Ron Paul, understands this. Even those strongly opposed to the war, such as Congressman John Murtha, advocate "repositioning" our troops, a mantra that keeps being repeated. In some cases the politicians seem to be talking about moving the troops to self-contained bases in Iraq or in Kurdistan. In other cases "reposition" means moving the troops over the horizon to the Persian Gulf. If the idea, however, is to secure peace and stop terrorist attacks on the U.S., keeping our troops in the Middle East will fail. It will only generate more terrorism. We must pull our soldiers back to the United States and stop trying to police the world.

The United States Can Still Succeed in Iraq

Frederick W. Kagan and Kimberly Kagan

*Frederick W. Kagan is a resident scholar at the American Enter-
prise Institute, a conservative public policy group. Kimberly Kagan is executive director of the Institute for the Study of War, a
private, nonpartisan group that focuses on providing information about military affairs.*

Iraq [is] a land caught between al-Qaeda terrorists and
Iranian-supported Shiite extremists. Iraq is a country facing
a complex set of challenges, run by imperfect leaders with
various agendas, protected by many courageous security forces
hindered by sectarian elements among them. It is a country in
which American forces are essential to establishing and securing order and are succeeding in that task. It is a country
where there are no easy solutions, but where success is possible if Americans and Iraqis show the necessary determination and skill. . . .

---

*[Iraq] is a country where there are no easy solutions, but
where success is possible if Americans and Iraqis show
the necessary determination and skill.*

The U.S. Role in Iraq

In Iraq, terrorists and militias are perpetrating sectarian violence, which is not otherwise endemic to modern Iraqi society. Iraqi Sunni and Shiites have lived together for generations, in cities and in rural areas, and have intermarried.

Frederick W. Kagan and Kimberly Kagan, "Iraq As It Is . . . and Not As Individuals
Might Have It Be," *National Review*, vol. 59, June 11, 2007, p. 33. Copyright © 2007
by National Review, Inc., 215 Lexington Avenue, New York, NY 10016. Reproduced by
permission.

Partition will not be possible without the forced movement of hundreds of thousands of people, many of whom do not want to move. And partition would be unstable. Both Sunnis and Shiites believe that they have a right to part of Baghdad. Fighting after partition would be at least as great as it was in 2006, and it would become endemic.

The trouble is not that Iraq's communities hate each other. Rampant violence between Sunnis and Shiites in Iraq did not erupt until February 2006, even though Sunni insurgents had been fighting coalition forces for several years and Abu Musab al-Zarqawi, the leader of al-Qaeda in Iraq, had stated his determination to incite sectarian violence in early 2004. He finally succeeded by destroying one of the holiest Shiite mosques. Since then, al-Qaeda and other Sunni extremist groups have targeted the residents of mixed neighborhoods, Shiite neighborhoods, and even purely Sunni neighborhoods. These terrorists have kidnapped and killed innocent Shiites in order to drive Shiite families from their homes alongside Sunni neighbors. Extreme cells of Shiite militias, in turn, have kidnapped and executed Sunni men, women, and children in order to displace residents from the neighborhoods where they have lived intermixed with Shiites.

For this reason, American troops must protect Iraqi civilians from violence, as they are doing now. The al-Qaeda and Shiite militias do not attack each other; they attack each other's innocent populations. Coalition operations to prevent such killings have been successful: Since Operation Enforcing the Law began on February 14 [2007], execution-style killings have fallen by two-thirds. American troops and American reconstruction efforts have enabled some markets in Baghdad to reopen, and economic and social life to resume along streets recently occupied by terrorists or militias. For example, significant U.S. forces fought al-Qaeda and other terrorists along Haifa Street in a series of multi-day combats in January 2007. American troops expelled those violent groups and patrol the area regularly. The market around the corner from Haifa Street is now flourishing. Sunnis and Shiites shop there. Their children play alongside the stalls.

American troops must protect Iraqi civilians from violence. . . . Al-Qaeda and Shiite militias do not attack each other; they attack each other's innocent populations.

American troops now stand not between warring communities, but between innocent Iraqi civilians and violent groups. If America backs off from this effort, the militias will be killing civilians on a larger scale. If America withdraws from Iraq outright, the neighboring states will probably intervene to try to fill the power vacuum. When we visited Iraq recently, one Iraqi general told us, "No true Iraqi citizen wants American forces to leave Iraq. Only terrorists and militias want the Americans to leave."

The Locals Have Their Own Problems

Iraq's leaders face tough problems that concern the survival of their state: how to reform the constitution, how to distribute power among groups, which groups should share in political power, what the rights of the majority and the minority should be. They are making these decisions not in peace and security, but in the crisis of wartime. Iraqi leaders also must develop the power and capacity of their government to provide services and enforce the law, while terrorists and militias actively attempt to undermine the government and destroy Iraq's ailing infrastructure. These problems would be challenges in any system, and even for the greatest and most experienced statesmen.

Experienced statesmen do not run Iraq. The current government took office only [in 2006]. Almost all of its leaders are new to governing, because the Iraqi constitution prevents the Baath party members who ran Saddam Hussein's bureaucracies from participating in the current government.

Iraqi institutions make resolving these complex problems harder. The current constitution is imperfect. The office of the prime minister [PM] lacks power—ministers do not serve at the pleasure of the prime minister as in most parliamentary systems. Nor does the PM control an effective majority in the Council of Representatives, so he cannot move legislation reliably; because of the sectarian distribution of offices, his political opponents operate within the government. Many elected leaders represent narrow sectarian interests, rather than the interests of the majority of the inhabitants of a city or province. Militias respond to a variety of leaders, but the PM does not have a militia of his own; he is handicapped, therefore, in dealing with the fact that others in his government can wield force to their own ends.

Iraq's leaders face pressures from many sides. The American political and military presence prevents the Iraqi government from caving entirely to the pressures of sectarian leaders or collapsing in the face of extensive violence. Far from allowing Iraqi leaders to avoid tough choices, America's military presence helps Iraqi leaders make the hard decisions. A withdrawal of U.S. forces will only leave the government of Iraq vulnerable to militias, terrorists, and aggressive neighbors.

The American . . . military presence prevents the Iraqi government from caving entirely to . . . sectarian leaders or collapsing in the face of extensive violence.

Not Ready Yet

The Iraqi security forces are not yet ready to defend the Iraqi people from sophisticated, well-organized, well-armed enemies. They depend on American forces for logistics, communications, air support, and artillery support. America cannot build these capacities within the Iraqi military overnight. Furthermore, secret cells of Shiite extremists have infiltrated some of the Iraqi security forces and have been kidnapping and killing innocent civilians in order to advance their sectarian agenda. The U.S. has an obligation to protect Iraqis from sectarian killing, while destroying these secret cells, as it has begun to do. Well-led Iraqi forces are assisting the U.S. in its efforts to rid Iraq of the militias preying on the population. Recent operations in [the Iraq city of] Diwaniyah, conducted by the Eighth Iraqi Army Division with the support of U.S. and Polish forces, exemplify the skills of well-trained, nonsectarian Iraqi army units. The Iraqi army is stepping up; but it cannot act alone.

The Iraqi security forces are not yet ready to defend the Iraqi people from sophistacted, well-organized, well-armed enemies. They depend on American forces.

Iran is supplying the most lethal weapons being used against American soldiers: explosively formed projectiles (EFPs), the signature explosive that Shiite militias emplace along roadways to destroy U.S. vehicles and kill U.S. soldiers. Iran is training some Shiite militias and their leaders in Iran and providing advisers to these groups within Iraq. Iran is also training—and perhaps supplying—some Sunni terrorist groups. Iran is thus funding competing militias and political parties.

Diplomatic negotiations between the U.S. and Iran will not solve these problems. Iran has faced a grave strategic threat from Iraq for decades. It is in Iran's interests to foment instability and a weak state in Iraq; or else to exert enough power that Iraq's government serves Iran's interests; or else actually to gain enough military power to overwhelm Iraq and other states in the region. America's interests are exactly contrary to Iran's. There is little room for compromise. And there is no reason for Iran to compromise as long as American defeat in Iraq appears possible. The U.S. will continue to lack leverage with which to negotiate until we have succeeded in Iraq and restored some measure of balance to the region.

America Can Still Succeed

America can still succeed in Iraq. Al-Qaeda and other extremist groups have attempted to terrorize Iraq's Sunni population into supporting their extremist interpretation of Islam. Most Sunni communities in Iraq have rejected this. In Anbar province, where the Sunni insurgency flourished from 2003 to 2006, tribal sheiks are expelling al-Qaeda. Their sons are joining the Iraqi security forces by the thousands. The anti-al-Qaeda movement is spreading into other Sunni provinces, such as Salah-ad-Din, and into mixed provinces, such as Diyala. American forces are helping the government of Iraq provide services, such as fuel distribution, to these areas. American forces are helping these communities secure themselves. American forces are establishing local governments. American forces are trying to establish a system of provincial elections that will give the Sunnis a share of power and a chance to participate in governing Iraq.

American political leaders must formulate policies based on ground truth, not on their imaginations. . . . Iraq . . . is real, filled with people and problems too complex to legislate from 6,000 miles away. American policymakers must debate and discuss the situation as it is. This debate requires a sophisticated and sustained effort to understand the actual situation in Iraq. There are no simple solutions to the problems in Iraq. America's presence advances, though it does not guarantee, the creation of a stable government for all Iraqis. America's presence prevents widespread sectarian cleansing. America's presence gives the Iraqi government an opportunity to grow in capacity and resolve political problems peacefully. Time, patience, and the establishment of security lay the groundwork for complex political negotiations and compromises. Setting timelines or withdrawing American forces will not pressure Iraqis to make tough decisions. It will guarantee failure.

The 2007 U.S. Troop Surge in Iraq Is Making Progress

Max Boot

Max Boot is a senior fellow at the Council on Foreign Relations, an independent, nonpartisan organization that promotes under-standing of U.S. foreign policy. He is also a contributing editor to the Weekly Standard, *a conservative magazine, and author of the 2006 book* War Made New: Technology, Warfare, and the Course of History, 1500 to Today.

Since February [2007], General David Petraeus and his team in Baghdad have been implementing classic counterinsurgency precepts that have worked wherever they have been tried in adequate strength over a sustained period of time—from the Philippines and South Africa in the early 1900s to Malaya in the 1950s, El Salvador in the 1980s, and Northern Ireland in the 1990s. They are surging more troops into troubled areas and pushing them off the remote fortress-like Forward Operating Bases and into neighborhoods where they conduct foot patrols, erect concrete barriers, and establish a street-level sense of security. The situation in Anbar province has improved substantially, and, while the areas around Baghdad remain deeply troubled, there are signs of progress in the capital itself. (Sectarian murders are down two-thirds since January [2007], though deaths from spectacular suicide bombings remain high.)

Where such strategies have worked, the results were achieved in years, not months. The same is likely true of Iraq, so patience remains the order of the day. But while Petraeus has the fundamentals right, there are still reforms that could be implemented to improve the odds of success. During a recent two-week visit with U.S. forces in Iraq, I saw a number of problems that need fixing, starting with the inadequate size of the Iraqi army.

Improving the Iraqi Army

The army is the most effective and nonsectarian institution in Iraq. Although it has its share of woes, its combat performance has been improving, and it is less corrupt than the police. But it's too small. Saddam Hussein kept more than 900,000 men under arms at the time of the 1991 Gulf war, a figure that had shrunk to fewer than 400,000 by the time of the U.S. invasion in 2003. Today the Iraqi army is only 136,000 strong. (There are another 194,000 police officers and 125,000 Facility Protection Service personnel, but many of them are useless or worse.) There is talk within the Iraqi Ministry of Defense and the American high command of expanding the Iraqi army by 35,000 to 40,000 soldiers a year for the next three years, but even this isn't enough. The army needs to be at least 300,000–400,000 strong. . . .

In walking the line between excessive lenience and excessive brutality, the Iraqi government needs to build more prisons.

Recruiting hasn't been a problem, not when unemployment is 20 percent or more. But it still may make sense to introduce conscription—something that is alien to currently serving American soldiers, all of whom are volunteers, but that has a long history in Iraq and neighboring states. An army in a developing nation like Iraq isn't there merely to fight internal and external enemies. Its mission is also to inculcate a civic religion of nationalism and egalitarianism in its recruits. Germany, Japan, Turkey, and other newly created states in the 19th and early 20th centuries turned the army into a "schoolhouse of the nation." That requires exposing a large percentage of young men to army training and indoctrination, not just a handpicked few. Iraq could usefully emulate their example, even if it does run the risk that, as in those societies, the army could become the ultimate arbiter of political power.

Expanding the army will require more money, and the United States should probably increase its military-assistance spending, but the Iraqis are starting to help themselves as well. [In 2007], for the first time, the Iraqi government is spending more on its security services (some $9 billion) than the amount of U.S. aid ($5 billion), and the Ministry of Defense has managed to spend 90 percent of its budget, which puts it well ahead of the curve in the semi-functional Maliki government. In any case, the cost of draftee soldiers would be less than that of volunteers, since they wouldn't have to be offered as much pay or benefits; they could also be employed with fewer restrictions on where and when they serve.

An expansion of the Iraqi army will also require an expansion of the number and quality of American advisers, which should not be that great a stretch, since even Democrats say they want to continue the advisory effort indefinitely. But while increasing support for the Iraqi security forces—and working hard to promote evenhanded, effective commanders—it is important to resist the temptation to impose our standards in all matters great and small. American advisers may unwittingly hold back the Iraqis in some instances by insisting they conform to the extraordinarily stringent standards of the U.S. armed forces—rules that, in terms of ethical conduct, are probably a good deal stricter than those previously employed by any army sent to quell any major insurgency in the long history of warfare. . . .

More Prisons

In walking the line between excessive lenience and excessive brutality, the Iraqi government needs to build more prisons.

The U.S. armed forces have been expanding capacity at their two main holding facilities, Camp Cropper in Baghdad and Camp Bucca in southern Iraq. The total prison population, which stood at less than 15,000 [in 2006], is now 19,000, and the plan is to expand to 25,000–30,000 by the end of the summer [2007], when the Baghdad security plan will be in full swing. The number of detainees held in Iraqi custody is unknown but estimated at perhaps 20,000. It's not enough. As military analysts Bing West and Eliot Cohen wrote not long ago, "One in 75 American males is in jail, compared to one in 450 Iraqi males." Since, as they note, "Iraq is not six times safer than the United States," the disparity needs to be addressed if Iraq is to become substantially more peaceful.

Part of the answer is to help the Iraqis build more prisons and appoint more judges. The coalition's Rule of Law Project is doing just that by constructing a facility within the Green Zone that will house not only 6,000 prisoners but also the judges who will try their cases. This is necessary to prevent intimidation of judges, which is said to be widespread and which results in "not guilty" verdicts in many cases in which U.S. troops are convinced the evidence is overwhelming.

Another necessity is to go more aggressively after foreign fighters ... [who] account for ... 80 to 90 percent of all suicide bombings.

Pursue Insurgents

But it is doubtful that any civilian legal system, much less one as anemic as Iraq's, could cope with the demands of wartime. The obvious answer is selective use of martial law to quell violence, giving authority to sentence insurgents to the same people who are risking their lives to catch them—Iraqi and American army officers. This would, of course, be controversial within Iraq. And since the United States is no longer an occupying power, we cannot impose martial law ourselves, but we could make it one of the points on which we lobby the Maliki government for results.

Next, create a readily accessible national identity database. This is an essential prerequisite for a successful counterinsurgency, yet it has never been implemented in Iraq, because successive American commanders have never thought they would be in the country long enough to pull off a project that might require a minimum of six to twelve months to implement. U.S. and Iraqi troops trying to identify potential insurgents have to rely either on food rationing cards, many of which are out of date and all of which lack biometric data such as fingerprints, or on their own haphazard surveys. Unfortunately, most of the data that U.S. troops amass during their tours of duty is lost when they rotate home. There is no uniform database to share population information among all security forces, American and Iraqi, current and future. Thus it's hard to know if someone stopped at a checkpoint belongs in the neighborhood or whether he is a wanted terrorist from another province. This is the kind of information that any U.S. cop would have available within seconds of a traffic stop, because he would run a check via a wireless computer terminal on the motorist's license plate and driver's license. Security forces need to have this same capability in Iraq. There is talk now within the Iraqi government of implementing such a system, but given the Maliki administration's lack of capacity, nothing meaningful will happen unless the Americans do it themselves.

Another necessity is to go more aggressively after foreign fighters. They comprise a relatively small percentage of the overall insurgency, but they account for a very high percentage of the most grotesque attacks—80 to 90 percent of all suicide bombings according to General Petraeus's briefing with Pentagon reporters on April 26 [2007]. These jihadists are of many nationalities, but most infiltrate from Syria. The Bush administration has repeatedly vowed that Syria would suffer unspecified consequences if it did not cut off this terrorist pipeline, but so far this has been an empty threat. The administration has refused to authorize Special Operations forces to hit terrorist safe houses and "rat lines" on the Syrian side of the border, even though international law recognizes the right of "hot pursuit" and holds states liable for letting their territory be used to stage attacks on neighbors. It's high time to unleash our covert operators—Delta Force [an army counterterrorism force], the SEALs [a navy sea, air and land special operations unit], and other units in the Joint Special Operations Command—to take the fight to the enemy. They can stage low-profile raids with great precision, and Syrian president Bashar Assad would have scant ability to retaliate. We also need to apply greater pressure to Iran, which continues to support both Shiite and Sunni terrorist groups in Iraq, but that will be harder to do because Tehran is a more formidable adversary than Damascus.

Improve U.S. Effectiveness

There are some less urgent moves than those above, which still might significantly improve our effectiveness in Iraq. It would be helpful to streamline the U.S. command structure. At the moment there are a bewildering variety of senior headquarters in Iraq: Multi-National Force-Iraq (MNFI, the four-star command in charge of overall strategy), Multi-National Corps-Iraq (MNCI, the three-star command in charge of day-to-day operations), and Multi-National Security Transition Command-Iraq (MNSTCI, the three-star command in charge of training and equipping Iraqi security forces). In addition, many of the functions performed by these military staffs (e.g., economic aid, legal affairs, contracting, public affairs, liaison with the Iraqi government) are also carried out by diplomats at the world's largest American embassy. And that's to say nothing of the parallel, often Byzantine structure of the Iraqi government.

The senior American leaders in Iraq today—General David Petraeus of MNFI, Lieutenant General Ray Odierno of MNCI, Lieutenant General Martin Dempsey of MNSTCI, and Ambassador Ryan Crocker—seem to be working fairly well together, but that wasn't always the case among their predecessors. And in any case, no matter how much goodwill there is at the top, the overlap between staffs can cause needless duplication and confusion. One recently returned army officer who served as an adviser to Iraqi troops complained to me that he was never sure who he was supposed to report to: Both MNSTCI and MNCI had jurisdiction over him.

U.S. forces are forbidden to conduct information operations on the Internet—the jihadists' favorite venue.

A more serious problem is that rebuilding projects undertaken by the U.S. Agency for International Development, the State Department, the Army Corps of Engineers, and their assorted contractors have often not been well coordinated with the pacification efforts of American combat troops. That's why so many projects have turned into white elephants—they were built in areas that didn't have a modicum of security. This problem is starting to be addressed by the embedding of the State Department's Provincial Reconstruction Teams within U.S. brigades, but greater efforts should be made to streamline and rationalize operations so as to further the essential principle of unity of command.

An Iraqi version of CORDS (Civil Operations and Rural Development Support) might help here. This was the agency created in 1967 under the leadership of "Blowtorch Bob" Komer. A veteran of the CIA and the National Security Council, Komer coordinated all civilian pacification efforts in Vietnam. He and his successor, William Colby, reported to the four-star commander of the U.S. Military Assistance Command, Vietnam, thus tying civil and military efforts closely together.

Information Operations

As part of a broader administrative overhaul, it would make sense to put more emphasis on "information operations" and to push these efforts down to lower levels of command. There is widespread agreement within the U.S. military that the war for hearts and minds is essential, and that so far al Qaeda and other jihadist groups have done a more effective job than the United States of competing in the "information battlespace." They are able to get their messages out more quickly and to make a bigger splash. Part of this is due to the natural disparity between a ruthless foe that can lie with impunity and intimidate the press and a democratic government that must tell the truth and not interfere with the free functioning of the media. But part of the disparity is also due to self-inflicted wounds on the part of the U.S. government.

I was stunned to learn in Iraq that leaflets and radio broadcasts need to be approved at the division level, and that press releases need to be approved one step higher, at the corps level. Even more amazing was the revelation that U.S. forces are forbidden to conduct information operations on the Internet—the jihadists' favorite venue—because of concerns at the highest levels of the U.S. government that American propaganda might inadvertently be seen by U.S. citizens browsing the web. Several junior officers told me that they have the authority to call in an airstrike that will kill dozens of people but not the authority to issue a press release. That's crazy. The authority to conduct public affairs and information operations needs to be pushed down to the level of the battalion and even the company, and American commanders at those levels and above need to be graded on their success in engaging in this all-important battleground.

Improve Accountability

Accountability should extend far beyond information operations, of course. There needs to be a much greater effort to promote good commanders and weed out bad ones. Imagine how poorly the Union would have fared in the Civil War if Lincoln had not cashiered McClellan, Pope, Hooker, Burnside, and numerous other ineffectual generals, while promoting Sherman, Grant, and Sheridan. President Bush has singularly failed to hold his commanders accountable. Lieutenant Colonel Paul Yingling, a veteran of two combat tours in Iraq, rightly complains in the new issue of *Armed Forces Journal* that, "as matters stand now, a private who loses a rifle suffers far greater consequences than a general who loses a war." Yingling isn't the only one upset by this. I've talked to many serving soldiers who are still fuming over the Medals of Freedom given to General Tommy Franks, Ambassador L. Paul Bremer III, and CIA director George Tenet—well-intentioned men all, but their medals were seen as a reward for failure. There was also a fair amount of grumbling within the ranks when the previous commander of U.S. forces in Iraq, General George Casey, was appointed Army chief of staff notwithstanding the deteriorating security situation on his watch.

Failed commanders ought to be fired or pushed aside, following the example of Major General Lloyd Fredendall, who was relieved after the debacle at Kasserine Pass in 1943 and replaced by George S. Patton Jr. Equally important, those who prove their mettle on the battlefield should be quickly promoted. At the moment, battalion and brigade commanders— the key combat leaders in this decentralized war—cycle through Iraq on their 6–7 month (Marine) or 12–15 month (Army) tours, and then proceed with the normal course of their careers. The successful ones may eventually be rewarded with promotion over their less successful colleagues, but the process will take years to play out. Given that we're at war, it would make sense to modify the peacetime personnel system and to resurrect the 19th-century practice of giving brevet ranks or field promotions to outstanding officers who have proven their merit in combat.

Of course, we could achieve an acceptable outcome in Iraq even without taking some of these steps. Conversely, we could lose even if we implement all of these recommendations. But the more of them we implement, the easier the job will become—and the greater the likelihood of success.

The Bush Administration Is Building an Embassy and Permanent Bases in Iraq to Protect U.S. Interests There

Kevin Zeese

Kevin Zeese is director of Democracy Rising, an antiwar organization, and ran an unsuccessful U.S. Senate campaign in Maryland for the 2006 elections.

The message is clear. Indeed, it's gigantic for all Iraqis, for the entire world to see. A 100-acre compound—ten times the size of the typical U.S. embassy, the size of 80 football fields, six times larger than the UN, the size of Vatican City. The U.S. Embassy Compound, in the middle of Baghdad—the center for U.S. domination of the Middle East and its resources. The compound towers above the Tigris River like a modern fortress. It will have its own sources of power and water and sit in the heart of Baghdad. If there is any thought that the U.S. is planning on leaving Iraq, the new embassy should make it clear 'We're staying!'

The growing skyline of the U.S. embassy in Baghdad is only the most recent indication that the U.S. has no intention of leaving. President [George W.] Bush has already told us we're there until the end of his tenure. More important than words, building "permanent" military bases in Iraq re-enforces the message of the huge embassy.

The DoD [the U.S. Department of Defense] does not like to use the word 'permanent' even for our bases in Germany and Korea. Euphemisms like "enduring bases" or "contingency operating bases" are used. They're less likely than 'permanent'

Kevin Zeese, "We're Staying! Unless the Iraqis Force the United States Out, The Evidence Shows the U.S. Isn't Leaving," *http://democracyrising.us*, April 21, 2006. Reproduced by permission.

to cause further anti-American unrest in Iraq. Brig. Gen. Mark Kimmitt, deputy chief of operations for the coalition in Iraq, told the *Chicago Tribune* in March 2004: "This is a blueprint for how we could operate in the Middle East." Zoltan Grossman, a geographer at Evergreen State College in Olympia, Wash., told the *Christian Science Monitor* . . . that since the fall of the Berlin Wall in 1989 the U.S. has established a string of 35 new bases between Poland and Pakistan, not including the Iraqi bases. He maintains the U.S. is establishing a "sphere of influence" in that region. The *Monitor* also reports that Joseph Gerson, author of *The Sun Never Sets: Confronting the Network of Foreign U.S. Military Bases,* says the war and bases aim at maintaining U.S. control over the Middle East with its massive oil resources.

An Expensive Plan

The plan entails construction of long-lasting facilities in Iraq. The bases will include barracks and offices built of concrete blocks, rather than metal trailers and tents. The buildings are designed to withstand direct mortar strikes. Initial funding was provided in the $82 billion supplemental appropriations bill approved by Congress in May 2005.

The *Christian Science Monitor* reported in April 2006, [that] "the Pentagon would prefer to keep its bases in Iraq. It has already spent $1 billion or more on them, outfitting some with underground bunkers and other characteristics of long-term bases. Some US bases in Iraq are huge, e.g., Camp Anaconda, north of Baghdad, occupies 15 square miles, boasts two swimming pools, a gym, a miniature-golf course, and a first-run movie theater. The $67.6 billion emergency bill to cover Iraq and Afghanistan military costs includes $348 million for further base construction."

According to Global Security Watch [a Web site that provides military information], on March 23, 2004 "it was reported that 'U.S. engineers are focusing on constructing 14 enduring bases,' long-term encampments for the thousands of American troops expected to serve in Iraq for at least two years. The US plans to operate from former Iraqi bases in Baghdad, Mosul, Taji, Balad, Kirkuk and in areas near Nasiriyah, near Tikrit, near Fallujah and between Irbil and Kirkuk ... [and to] enhance airfields in Baghdad and Mosul ..."

The infrastructure is being put in place for a long-term military presence in Iraq. Unless Americans get tired of footing the growing and expensive bill for occupying Iraq ... or the Iraqis are able to force the United States to leave...

Long-lasting military bases in Iraq will be an expensive budget item even if the U.S. decides to reduce its forces to 50,000, less than half the current troop level. The annual cost would run between $5 billion [and] $7 billion a year, estimates *Gordon Adams*, director of *Security Policy Studies* at George Washington University in Washington, D.C. [In June 2006], the House voted, by a voice vote, to oppose a permanent military presence in Iraq. Future on the record votes for appropriations will show whether this was a symbolic election-year vote, or something the House is serious about.

Part of the U.S. Plan

President George W. Bush claims [the] U.S. only intends to stay "as long as necessary and not one day more." And, former Secretary of [Defense] Donald Rumsfeld has testified on February 17, 2005 in Congress: "I can assure you that we have no intention at the present time of putting permanent bases in Iraq." These claims are hard to believe when Congress voted for the first funds for long-term bases that May, and construction is now underway.

As *Joost Hiltermann*, of the International Crisis Group, said: "One of the reasons they invaded, as far as I can tell, is because they needed to shift their military operation from Saudi Arabia, and Iraq was probably the easiest one in terms of a big country to support their presence in the Gulf." Also, the idea that the U.S. wanted to swap Iraq for Saudi Arabia was acknowledged by then-deputy secretary of defense Paul Wolfowitz in an interview with *Vanity Fair* in 2003 saying: ". . . we can now remove almost all of our forces from Saudi Arabia. Their presence there over the last 12 years has been a source of enormous difficulty for a friendly government. It's been a huge recruiting device for al Qaeda."

On April 20, 2003 *The New York Times* reported "the U.S. is planning a long-term military relationship with the emerging government of Iraq, one that would grant the Pentagon access to military bases and project American influence into the heart of the unsettled region."

In May 2005 the *Washington Post* reported that plans called for consolidating American troops in Iraq into four large air bases: Tallil in the south, Al Asad in the west, Balad in the center and either Irbil or Qayyarah in the north. Each base would support a brigade combat team, along with aviation and other support personnel.

In January 2005 it was reported that the Pentagon was building a permanent military communications system in Iraq. The new Central Iraq Microwave System, is to consist of up to 12 communications towers throughout Iraq, along with fiber-optic cables connecting Camp Victory to other coalition bases in the country. The U.S. also has plans to renovate and enhance airfields in Baghdad and Mosul, and rebuild 70 miles of road on the main route for U.S. troops headed north.

The infrastructure is being put in place for a long-term military presence in Iraq. Unless Americans get tired of footing the growing and expensive bill for occupying Iraq—now at nearly $10 billion per month—or the Iraqis are able to force the United States to leave it looks like Baghdad will be the center of operations for the U.S. presence in the Middle East. The U.S. will be sitting on top of the Earth's vast, but shrinking, oil resources.

CHAPTER 3

Can the Israeli-Palestinian Conflict Be Resolved?

Chapter Preface

Throughout the many decades of the Arab-Israeli conflict, a group called Fatah (an acronym for an Arabic name) has been the main Palestinian advocate for an independent Palestinian nation. Fatah was founded in the 1950s and, after the 1967 Six-Day War between Israel and surrounding Arab countries, became part of the Palestine Liberation Organization (PLO), a confederation of nationalist groups headed by then Palestinian leader Yasser Arafat. Thereafter, Fatah carried out numerous airplane hijackings and terrorist attacks against Israeli targets as part of the PLO's resistance to Israeli occupation of Gaza and the West Bank—territories seized by Israel in the 1967 war. In the 1990s, however, Arafat and the PLO renounced terrorism, and Fatah became the dominant force in a Palestinian government that was set up to allow Palestinian self-rule in the occupied territories. Palestinians hoped Fatah, at this point supported by the U.S. government, would eventually negotiate a peace treaty with Israel that would create a Palestinian state.

But as the years passed with no progress in peace negotiations, the Palestinian people began to lose faith in Fatah. Fatah politicians also were increasingly criticized for financial corruption and mismanagement. These frustrations were finally released in January 2006, when Palestinian voters in democratic legislative elections rejected the Fatah party, then led by Palestinian president Mahmoud Abbas, and voted instead for an Islamist group called Hamas (an acronym meaning "Islamic Resistance Movement"). Hamas is considered by the United States and others to be a terrorist group and much more militant than Fatah ever was. Hamas historically has refused to recognize Israel's right to exist as a nation and is dedicated to fostering fundamentalist Islamic rule not only in Palestinian areas but throughout the Middle East.

The Hamas election victory set up a power struggle between it and Fatah party leaders, including President Abbas, who was elected in an earlier election to a four-year term. Although Hamas won a majority of the seats in the Palestinian Legislative Council, Fatah supporters continued to occupy many government posts and made up most of the Palestinian security forces, which are charged with keeping order in the Palestinian territories. In early 2007, Abbas and Hamas agreed to set up a unity government, but that effort proved fatally flawed. The two sides continued to engage in a political tug of war that, increasingly, erupted into actual fighting and street violence. Finally, in June 2007, Hamas fighters took control of Gaza, causing Fatah troops and politicians to flee the area. A Hamas spokesperson proclaimed: "The era of justice and Islamic rule have arrived." Abbas promptly dissolved the unity government and set up an emergency government, and many political commentators warned that a full-fledged Palestinian civil war could be the end result.

Perhaps surprisingly, U.S. officials may have welcomed the Fatah-Hamas fight. The election of Hamas shocked the United States and caused it and the European Union to cut their financial assistance to the Palestinian Authority, the government of the Palestinians, depriving them of almost a billion dollars of desperately needed funds and increasing the pressure on both parties. The United States also sent arms to Fatah and reportedly urged President Abbas to confront Hamas. Critics said U.S. officials sought to oust Hamas from the Palestinian government, perhaps because Hamas would be a tough negotiator in peace talks and had increasingly developed ties to al Qaeda, the Islamic terrorist group responsible for the September 11, 2001, attacks on America. Although the United States often claims to support democratically elected governments, in the case of Hamas, this support was withheld. The United States and Israel also refused to enter peace negotiations with Hamas, unless it first renounced all violence and agreed to recognize Israel.

Some commentators criticized this stance, arguing that the United States and Israel instead should have sought to negotiate peace terms with Hamas, the elected representative of the Palestinian people. Hamas's entry into mainstream politics, these analysts argued, might have helped the group to eventually moderate its policies. Critics also pointed to the fact that Hamas leader Khalid Mechal stated that Hamas would be willing to negotiate with Israel, if Israel agreed to a series of conditions, one of which was withdrawing to its 1967 borders, which would mean leaving the Israeli-occupied Arab territories of Gaza, the West Bank, and the Golan Heights. This Hamas offer was summarily rejected by Israel and U.S. officials. The result was a stalemate in peace negotiations and mounting frustration among Palestinians.

The situation of divided government now facing the Palestinians and the world, many observers say, has only created new obstacles for the Middle East peace process and more misery for Palestinians. With Hamas controlling Gaza, Fatah still in charge of the West Bank, and an ongoing struggle for power, no one knows whether a Palestinian unity government can ever be resurrected. And although U.S. and European officials decided to resume financial aid to Abbas's emergency government, it is uncertain how Abbas will be able to effectively govern when his party lacks the support of most Palestinians. Meanwhile, Gaza seems destined to become more isolated and may become a base for even more violent Hamas terrorist strikes against Israel.

On the other hand, the crisis in Gaza may set the stage for a new round of peace negotiations. With Hamas isolated, U.S. and Israeli leaders appear ready to explore renewed peace talks. Also, former British prime minister Tony Blair has been named a special international envoy to the region by the diplomatic Quartet—a group of four political entities that includes the United States, the European Union, Russia, and the United Nations. Some commentators suggest that Israel and the international community may fear Hamas enough to finally push for a fair and final peace settlement for the region.

Although Arab-Israeli relations have clearly deteriorated because of these events, in mid-2007, the underlying issues in the peace process remain largely the same. The authors in this chapter highlight these various outstanding issues and give their views on the chances for a final resolution to the conflict.

The Arab-Israeli Conflict Can Be Resolved

International Crisis Group

International Crisis Group is an independent nonprofit, nongovernmental organization that works to prevent and resolve deadly conflicts throughout the world.

With the Middle East immersed in its worst crisis for years, we call for urgent international action towards a comprehensive settlement of the Arab-Israeli conflict. Everyone has lost in this conflict except the extremists throughout the world who prosper on the rage that it continues to provoke. Every passing day undermines prospects for a peaceful, enduring solution. As long as the conflict lasts, it will generate instability and violence in the region and beyond.

Outlines for a Peace Agreement

The outlines of what is needed are well known, based on UN Security Council resolutions 242 of 1967 and 338 of 1973, the Camp David peace accords of 1978, the Clinton Parameters of 2000, the Arab League Initiative of 2002, and the Roadmap [a peace plan] proposed in 2003 by the Quartet [a group that includes the United Nations, United States, European Union, and Russia]. The goal must be security and full recognition to the state of Israel within internationally recognized borders, an end to the occupation for the Palestinian people in a viable independent, sovereign state, and the return of lost land to Syria.

We believe the time has come for a new international conference, held as soon as possible and attended by all relevant players, at which all the elements of a comprehensive peace agreement would be mapped, and momentum generated for detailed negotiations.

Steps Toward Peace

Whether or not such an early conference can be convened, there are crucial steps that can and should be taken by the key players, including:

- Support for a Palestinian national unity government, with an end to the political and financial boycott of the Palestinian Authority.

- Talks between Israel and the Palestinian leadership, mediated by the Quartet and reinforced by the participation of the Arab League and key regional countries, on rapidly enhancing mutual security and allowing revival of the Palestinian economy.

- Talks between the Palestinian leadership and the Israeli government, sponsored by a reinforced Quartet, on the core political issues that stand in the way of achieving a final status agreement.

- Parallel talks of the reinforced Quartet with Israel, Syria and Lebanon, to discuss the foundations on which Israeli-Syrian and Israeli-Lebanese agreements can be reached.

Nobody underestimates the intractability of the underlying issues or the intensity of feelings they provoke. But if the Arab-Israeli conflict, with all its terrible consequences, is ever to be resolved, there is a desperate need for fresh thinking and the injection of new political will. The times demand no less.

The Palestinians Are Ready for Peace If Israel Will Negotiate

Daoud Kuttab

Daoud Kuttab is a Palestinian journalist and director of the Institute of Modern Media at Al-Quds University in Ramallah, the Palestinian capital city.

When [former U.S. secretary of state] Henry Kissinger coined the term "constructive ambiguity" during his attempts to negotiate Arab-Israeli peace, he couldn't have expected that one day Palestinians would use it in their own peace initiative. The ambiguity in the agenda of the new Palestinian "unity government" depends on whether one sees the cup as half full or half empty. If Israel and the United States want to move forward on the peace process, the cup is half full. But if there is no real will to pay the price for peace, the cup is half empty.

[In 2006], with international encouragement, the Palestinian people adopted electoral democracy, even before they enjoyed sovereignty and the end of the Israeli occupation. They threw out their longtime Fatah [a moderate Palestinian party] secularist leaders and replaced them with Hamas [a militant Islamic group]. The unjust freeze on Palestinian aid that followed sparked a social revolt and the beginnings of a civil war; this was stopped in part by . . . [a] Fatah-Hamas coalition that produced the unity government.

The Palestinians Are Ready for Peace

For the first time in the history of the Palestinian-Israeli conflict, a majority of Palestinians, including the Islamists, are willing to accept a Palestinian state within the internationally acceptable borders of 1967. The implicit recognition of Israel in this is supported by clauses in agreements between the Palestine Liberation Organization [PLO] and Israel that included mutual recognition as well as respect for Arab and international resolutions and treaties. By demanding explicit recognition before negotiations can begin, Israel and others are being unreasonable. No other people without sovereignty has been forced to recognize an occupier whose borders are vague. By accepting an independent state in the West Bank and Gaza [Palestinian territories occupied by Israel] alongside Israel, the Palestinians have declared the borders of their own state and offer the possibility of mutual recognition through negotiation.

It is time for Israel and the international community to . . . work toward peace.

Palestinian President Mahmoud Abbas, the supreme military commander, has called for an end to occupation through negotiations and has rejected outright the use of violence. While insisting on the people's right to resist occupation through any method, the unity government prioritizes nonviolent resistance. Furthermore, by seeking to extend the ceasefire in Gaza to the West Bank, the new government is offering an olive branch to the Israelis even before negotiations begin.

Politically, the new government provides a logical process regarding negotiations for a permanent resolution of the conflict. It gives Abbas and the PLO which he chairs, full authority to negotiate a peace agreement with Israel. Once an agreement is reached, it is to be ratified by the Palestinian National Council [the legislative body of the PLO] or through a referendum. Polls of Palestinians consistently show strong support for a peace based on the two-state solution. So an Abbas-brokered deal approved by the people is possible even with Hamas in power. Such a peace, negotiated by a moderate Palestinian and approved by the silent majority, would last. The alternative, making a secret deal without public support, would not last and would easily be torpedoed, as we saw with the Oslo accords.

The Half-Empty View

Opponents of peace find plenty of excuses to see the cup as half empty. The Palestinian prime minister, for one thing, belongs to an Islamic movement that has not yet declared its strategic long-term position regarding Israel. Those not interested in peace note that Hamas refuses to recognize Israel.

Hamas's supporters, however, note that it took the PLO 30 years to recognize Israel and that in the past 12 months, Hamas has come a long way by accepting the 1967 borders of a future Palestinian state. Hamas's commitment to the Gaza-only cease-fire also shows that it can be trusted to meet its obligations.

In June 1967, Israel occupied Palestinian and Arab lands. Forty years later, in defiance of U.N. resolutions, the Israeli army is still occupying the lands and oppressing the people, and the government still supports building illegal settlements in Palestinian territory. Soon after the occupation, the late [Israeli minister of defense] Moshe Dayan said that the Israelis were waiting for a phone call from any Arab leader. Instead, Arabs resolved not to recognize Israel, not to negotiate with Israel and not to make peace with Israel.

Since then, Palestinians and other Arabs have reversed themselves, offering peace, negotiations and recognition in return for Israeli withdrawal to the 1967 borders. The new Palestinian government ... will approve and reiterate the Arab peace initiative, first made in Beirut in 2002, that called for an exchange of land for recognition as well as normalization.

It is time for Israel and the international community to see that the cup is half full. By choosing to work toward peace, they can fill it the rest of the way—or stand by and watch the drops of hope dry up.

The Arab Peace Initiative Versus the Culture of Confrontation

Ami Isseroff

Ami Isseroff is director of MidEastWeb for Coexistence, a Web site that promotes dialogue and education about the Middle East and disseminates balanced news and views.

The Arab peace initiative, renewed at the recent Arab summit, has created the expected confusion in Israel. The doves, predictably, insist that Israel must seize the opportunity The Arab side has come a long way since the "three nos" of the Khartoum conference, and offers peace, as hardnosed Zeev Schiff notes. The offer cannot be dismissed easily. Even if it is a bad offer, the admission that Israel has the right to exist and that there could be peace in principle establishes a precedent, a change in the culture of the conflict, and it must not be ignored. From Israel's point of view, it is a giant step forward that should be amplified and bolstered in any way possible.

The Israeli government, for its part, sniffs and pokes at the peace initiative like a dog who is not too hungry and has been offered some strange food.

Dennis Ross is probably right that neither Olmert nor Abbas are strong enough to make peace, and that, in itself, tells us something about the current mentality of Israelis and Palestinians. If there was a proposal by the Saudi Arabians to grant each Palestinian and each Israeli and every Arab $100,000 each, neither Olmert nor Abbas nor Abdullah of Jordan would need to be "strong" to pass that motion. Money is desirable. Peace is better than money. It is life as well as prosperity. It is more important than holy rocks in Jerusalem and a Palestinian state with its capital in Jerusalem or settlements in Ariel and in Kiriat Kanaim and Maaleh Mitnahlim. It is more important then the right to "return" to where you have never been. However, among Israelis and Palestinians "Peace" is a dirty word. Peace initiatives are a foreign imposition to be dealt with by evasion and parrying, and by putting on a show of peace initiative for visiting dignitaries like Condoleezza Rice.

The novelty of the Saudi peace plan is that a major Middle East player has made a bid for leadership based on peace.

The antipathy to peace is due to cultural and geopolitical realities that cannot be dismissed. No peace plan can succeed as long as people do not really want peace, because the demands and requirements that they make are designed to prevent peace, and if those are met, they will find new ones. It is absolutely necessary to have a settlement in Ariel because having the settlement in Ariel will prevent the possibility of a viable Palestinian state. It is essential to get return of the Palestinian refugees to Israel, because return of the refugees to Israel will destroy the Jewish state. The geopolitical realities are such that at any given time there are a number of Middle East states, political groups and terrorist groups who compete for leadership in the Arab or Muslim world by exploiting the issue of the Israeli-Palestinian conflict. Nasser, Syria, PLO, Iraq under Saddam and now Iran, Syria, Hezbullah and Al-Qaedaa have all played the game. A miniature version of this game is played in Israeli politics. They all have a vested interest in preventing the peace, in instilling the idea that peace is treachery and concessions are disastrous. The warning of Israeli MK Bishara to the Hamas not to make any concessions is typical of this mentality. The political reality influences the hearts of the people and molds the culture of confrontation, and the culture of confrontation molds the politics of confrontation.

The novelty of the Saudi peace plan is that a major Middle East player has made a bid for leadership based on peace, and not on the politics of confrontation. This fact stands by itself, like Anwar Sadat's dramatic campaign, but the result must be judged in the context of the Middle East. Egypt did not become the leader of the Arab World by making peace with Israel. It was isolated, Sadat was assassinated, and Egypt withdrew into a cold peace. Peace cannot succeed until this reality is changed, because the spoilers can always blow up the peace process, as the Hamas did in 1996 and has been doing ever since.

The Arab peace initiative creates a diplomatic problem for Israel.

Many Israelis join Azmi Bishara in the refusal camp, continuing the politics of confrontation. They ask if the initiative is a Peace Plan or a Political Ploy. They believe that the Arab Peace Initiative is dangerous, because accepting it would imply that Israel accepts full withdrawal and return of the Palestinian refugees, and it is therefore designed to destroy Israel rather than to make peace.

Probably they are right, and those who argue that the peace initiative is a golden opportunity for Israel are also right, and those who argue that it is neither dangerous nor wonderful, but just empty words, may also be right. Everyone can be right about the Arab peace initiative, because it is a "consensus" document, a bit of constructive ambiguity. Like the manna that the Israelites ate in the Exodus, each person can taste what they want when eating it.

The Arab League is a conglomeration of states. The Saudis may propose the plan for one reason, while others may accept it for other reasons. The consensus was reached because all the Arab states benefit from this initiative, whether or not Israel accepts it. The Saudis get to lead the Arab world. The Arabs look good for the benefit of the Americans. The Syrians can use it to exert pressure to get back the Golan Heights. The Arabs also benefit from putting Iran on the spot regarding peace with Israel, and trying to isolate Hamas from Iran. Everyone gets something and nobody loses anything.

The precise meaning of the initiative is deliberately obscured, so that all the Arab states could agree to it, each with their very own interpretation. Some may believe that it implies that all Palestinian Arab refugees will return to Israel. All certainly believe that it demands Arab sovereignty over East Jerusalem. In some ways it is quite like the "peace offers" of 1949 that also demanded territorial concessions and return of large numbers of refugees, and were rejected by Israel.

For Israel, the danger of the Arab peace initiative is not what detractors insist that it is. The Arab peace initiative creates a diplomatic problem for Israel. It is a public peace offer—a "peace offensive" in all senses of the phrase. It is being given momentum and importance by the publicity attached to it by the Arab states, and by its strategic timing. The United States State Department believes that the key to its salvation in Iraq is solution of the Israeli-Palestinian conflict. This belief is encouraged by wording inserted in the Iraq Study Group (ISG) proposal. According to knowlegeable Washington sources, this wording was a last minute addition, added at the insistence of one individual, retired CIA analyst Ray Close, who was an ISG advisor. Such beliefs, whatever their truth value, can quickly become entrenched in Washington or in any other government, and form the basis of far-reaching policy decisions.

For over half a century, the Israeli-Arab conflict has been immune to solution. Now, at precisely the moment when the United States believes it is most urgent to resolve the problem, the Arabs offer a "philosophers' stone" that will ostensibly convert lead to gold, a solution to an impossible problem. Of course, the Americans must grasp this opportunity, however illusory it might be.

Even if it is completely meaningless, this new "peace offensive" can isolate Israel as the party, that is an "obstacle to peace." If it is not met appropriately, Israel will become public enemy number one in Washington and in European capitals as well. Israel will be viewed as blocking American salvation in Iraq, and endangering the price of oil as well. The Arabs have opened an important new front on the diplomatic battlefield, that attempts to flank Israeli positions. Our flanks are undefended.

There are indications indeed that the plan is just a device, a gimmick, that is not intended to be pursued seriously. Secretary Rice came to the Middle East full of naive American enthusiasm. She took the Arabs at their word, and wanted to set up a mini-conference to begin negotiating peace. This rosy exuberance was quickly cooled by King Abdullah of Jordan. After her visit to Jordan, there was no more talk of summits by Dr. Rice. This is the same Abdullah who had so recently toured the US pleading for peace.

In a news conference following the Arab League Summit, Prince Saud declared that there was nothing, in effect, for Israel to negotiate with most Arab countries. Israel should first meet all the forms of the Syrians, Palestinians and Lebanese, and then the Arab countries would make peace, at an unspecified date. Perhaps they would, and perhaps they would not. However, it is clear that Prince Saud is not stupid, and that he understands that Israel would not make sweeping concessions of the type demanded in the initiative unless there was absolute certainty that Israel will get peace from the Arabs in return. Moreover, the Arabs rejected Olmert's offer to meet and did not make a counter offer, so apparently they are not as anxious to make peace as to talk about making peace.

The terms of the initiative in their worst interpretation are certainly unacceptable to Israel, but Israel cannot afford to stand by and do nothing. Gimmick or not, the initiative is a very effective weapon in the diplomatic war that Arab countries have been waging against Israel. Whining that the initiative is not serious and ignoring it will not suffice.

It would be inappropriate for Israel to respond to this initiative with a simple "no" or with a half-hearted "let's talk" as Olmert has done. Vague talk of "political horizons" is not enough either. Israel must craft a public peace plan of its own and put it on the table to compete with the Arab Peace Initiative. This plan should reflect national consensus, and must be generous enough to get the backing of the European Union and the United States. For the Palestinians, it can be modeled on the Clinton Bridging Proposals or the Geneva Initiative or the Ayalon Nusseibeh plan. These are the plans that all the experts point to as the only possible shape of a peace solution: "two states for two peoples" and territorial compromise. None of these plans contemplate full withdrawal or massive return of Palestinian Arab refugees. All of them would give both sides peace with security, if they are carried out as agreed. All of them would safeguard Israeli rights in Jerusalem and other holy places to a greater or lesser extent, as well as allowing for Arab rights. Therefore, these plans can have a greater appeal to the international community than the Arab peace plan.

On the Israeli side, there must be realization that it is, after all, possible to make peace and desirable to do so.

The Arab peace initiative also demands that Israel negotiate peace with Syria. Israel should be asking loudly of the USA, or threatening to ask in public, if their support for the initiative means that the US wants Israel to begin negotiations with Syria. Apparently the USA does not want to say this, but if so, they should get Israel off the hook. Very likely, Mr. Bush doesn't want to say it, but Dr. Condoleezza Rice does want to say it. The Arab League is not the only forum with divergences of opinion.

Any public Israeli peace plan is better than no plan at all. There is not much to the Arab peace plan. Like any good military strategy, it is simple but deadly. The plan does not have to be complex. It might suffice for Israel to say that it accepts the principle of land for peace, and will make peace with all Arab countries based on UN Security Council Resolution 242 and the Bridging Proposals of President Clinton.

The Arab peace initiative is indeed dangerous. Israel must recognize that, in a sense, it is under attack, and that the attack must be met with a concrete public plan to match the Arab plan. This diplomatic attack is more dangerous and urgent than the helter-skelter Qassam rocket fire, and it can be more dangerous than the rockets of the Hezbullah. If not met, it can run out of Israeli supply lines from the USA and Europe and our diplomatic support from those countries, and that could really mean the end of Israel. If the "attack" is met it becomes an opportunity. Even if no peace agreement is reached immediately, it helps to legitimize two very important ideas that must be the basis of any future peace. On the Arab side, there must be an understanding that Israel is here to stay and that recognizing Israel and the rights of Jews is no longer a cultural taboo. On the Israeli side, there must be realization that it is, after all, possible to make peace and desirable to do so. Once both sides agree on both points, most of the solution is in hand.

Palestinians' Desire to Destroy Israel Prevents a Peaceful Settlement to the Arab–Israeli Conflict

Dennis Prager

Dennis Prager is a radio show host and a contributing columnist for Townhall.com, a conservative Web site that publishes political commentary of the nation's top radio personalities.

The Middle East conflict is difficult to solve, but it is among the simplest conflicts in history to understand. The Arab and other Muslim enemies of Israel (for the easily confused, this does not mean every Arab or every Muslim) want Israel destroyed. That is why there is a Middle East conflict. Everything else is commentary.

A History of Opposition to Israel

Those who deny this and ascribe the conflict to other reasons, such as "Israeli occupation," "Jewish settlements," a "cycle of violence," "the Zionist lobby" and the like, do so despite the fact that Israel's enemies regularly announce the reason for the conflict. The Iranian regime, Hizbollah [a militant Islamic group in Lebanon], Hamas [a militant Palestinian group] and the Palestinians—in their public opinion polls, in their anti-Semitic school curricula and media, in their election of Hamas, in their support for terror against Israeli civilians in pre-1967 borders—as well as their Muslim supporters around the world, all want the Jewish state annihilated.

In 1947–48, the Arab states tried to destroy the tiny Jewish state formed by the United Nations partition plan. In 1967,

Dennis Prager, "The Middle East Conflict Is Hard to Solve But Easy to Explain," *www .Townhall.com*, July 18, 2006. Copyright © 2006 by Creators Syndicate. Reproduced by permission.

Egypt, Syria and Jordan tried to destroy Israel in what became known as the Six-Day War. All of this took place before Israel occupied one millimeter of Palestinian land and before there was a single Jewish settler in the West Bank.

Two months after the Six-Day War of June 5–10, 1967, the Arab countries convened in Khartoum, Sudan, and announced on Sept. 1, 1967, their famous "Three NOs" to Israel: "No peace, No recognition, No negotiations."

Six years later, in 1973, Egypt invaded the Israeli-held Sinai Peninsula, a war that ended in a boost in Egyptian morale from its initially successful surprise attack. Though nearly all of the Sinai remained in Israel's hands, the boost in Egyptian self-confidence enabled Egypt's visionary president, Anwar Sadat, four years later (November 1977), to do the unimaginable for an Arab leader: He visited Israel and addressed its parliament in Jerusalem. As a result, in 1978, Israel and Egypt signed a peace treaty in return for which Israel gave all of the oil-rich Sinai Peninsula back to Egypt.

Three years later, in 1981, Sadat was assassinated by Egyptian Muslims, a killing welcomed by most Arabs, including the PLO (Palestine Liberation Organization). Why welcomed? Because Sadat had done the unforgivable—recognized Israel and made peace with it.

Give Israel peace, and Israel will give you land.

Israelis Ache for Peace

The lesson that Palestinians should have learned from the Israeli-Egyptian peace agreement was that if you make peace with Israel, you will not only get peace in return, you will also get all or nearly all of your land back. That is how much Israelis ache for peace.

Think about Israel for one moment: Israel is one of the most advanced countries on earth in terms of culture (most books published, translated from other languages and read per capita; most orchestras per capita, etc.); major advances in medicine; technological breakthroughs; and decency as a society, as exemplified by its treatment of its women, gays and even its large Arab minority (particularly remarkable in light of the widespread Arab and Muslim anti-Semitism and desire to annihilate Israel). This is hardly a picture of some bloodthirsty, land-grabbing society. And Jews, whatever their flaws, have never been known to be a violent people. If anything, the stereotypical Jew has been depicted as particularly docile.

As a lifelong liberal critic of Israeli policies, the *New York Times* foreign affairs columnist Thomas Friedman wrote . . . : "The Palestinians could have a state on the West Bank, Gaza and East Jerusalem tomorrow, if they and the Arab League clearly recognized Israel, normalized relations and renounced violence. Anyone who says otherwise doesn't know Israel today." Give Israel peace, and Israel will give you land.

The Failure of Camp David Peace Talks

Which is exactly what Israel agreed to do in the last year of the [U.S. president Bill] Clinton administration. It offered PLO Chairman Yasser Arafat about 97 percent of the West Bank and three percent of Israel's land in exchange for peace. Instead, Israel got its men, women and children routinely blown up and maimed by Palestinian terrorists after the Palestinians rejected the Israeli offer at Camp David [a U.S. presidential retreat in Maryland]. Even President Clinton, desirous of being the honest broker and yearning to be history's Middle East peacemaker, blamed the ensuing violence entirely on the Palestinians.

Israel's Camp David offer of a Palestinian state for Palestinian peace was rejected because most Palestinians and their Arab and Muslim supporters don't want a second state. They want Israel destroyed. They admit it. Only those who wish Israel's demise and the willfully naive do not.

If you don't believe this, ask almost anyone living in the Middle East why there is a Middle East War, preferably in Arabic. If you ask in English, they will assume you are either an academic, a Western news reporter, a diplomat or a "peace activist." And then, they will assume you are gullible and will tell you that it's because of "Israeli occupation" or "the Zionist [pro-Israel] lobby." But they know it isn't. And it never was.

American/Israeli Preconditions Have Blocked the Peace Process

Seth Ackerman

Seth Ackerman is a contributing writer to Fairness & Accuracy in Reporting (FAIR), a national media watchdog group.

Editor's Note: In June 2007, fighting between Hamas and Fatah, rival Palestinian groups, led to a divided Palestinian government, in which Hamas controls one of the Israeli-occupied territories, Gaza, while President Mahmoud Abbas and Fatah control another occupied territory, the West Bank.

Palestinian leaders [in 2007 formed] a national unity government to end the international siege that has crippled life in the occupied territories. But . . . the real decisions will be made in Washington.

Since Hamas' [a militant Islamic group] victory in January [2006 Palestinian] parliamentary elections, the policy of the "international community" has actually been set in the Oval Office [the U.S. president's office]. Diplomatic contacts have been frozen, peace talks are indefinitely deferred and international aid has been halted. Even as conditions deteriorate in the territories and fighting between Israel and Palestinian groups escalates, Washington insists there will be no change in policy until Hamas signs on to its famous three demands: It must recognize Israel, renounce violence and sign up to the Road Map [a peace proposal backed by the United States].

The media have portrayed [George W.] Bush's demands as a way of forcing Hamas to moderate its stance so that peace negotiations with Israel can resume. But the truth is almost exactly the opposite: Over the past year or two, Hamas' political leadership has pushed the movement towards an unprecedented degree of diplomatic flexibility, despite its continuing militant rhetoric. [In 2005], the party campaigned on a platform of supporting peace talks led by [Palestinian president Mahmoud] Abbas and party leaders have repeatedly pushed for a mutual cease-fire with Israel. While refusing to recognize Israel itself, Hamas' government program calls for a national referendum on any peace deal that grants recognition to the Jewish state.

The [George W.] Bush administration has deliberately set demands it knows Hamas can't swallow.

Unreasonable Demands to Block Peace

But that is precisely what worries Jerusalem and Washington. In any negotiations that happen while Hamas is in power, "the Palestinian positions will stiffen enormously," as *Ha'aretz*'s [an Israeli newspaper] Danny Rubinstein wrote [in 2005]. Yet with Bush's strong support, Israeli Prime Minister Ehud Olmert came into office with a plan to keep a permanent grip over East Jerusalem and the three large settlement blocs surrounding it, while evacuating the smaller isolated settlements in the West Bank. Whatever else it might support, Hamas would never give its consent to Olmert's plan.

Hamas' leadership has been deeply divided over just how far to go in softening the party's stance in exchange for international legitimacy and aid. The strategy of moderates like Prime Minister Ismail Haniyeh [a Hamas leader] has been to nudge the group as far as possible towards a tacit acceptance of Israel without provoking dissent from the group's more militant members. In exchange, he hopes to win recognition, aid and a period of calm, to prove to the hardliners in his own party that pragmatism will yield benefits. On a recent trip to London, Haniyeh's advisor, Ahmad Yousef, pitched the idea of a 10-year cease-fire with Israel. "We need to change people's minds on how they look at the conflict, and it will take time," he told *The Guardian*. "The climate will change if we have a period of peace."

But the [George W.] Bush administration has deliberately set demands it knows Hamas can't swallow. As *The New York Times* reported [in] February [2006], the U.S. officials who drafted the conditions "do not expect Hamas to meet them." Instead, they are determined to force out the elected Palestinian government—peacefully if possible, but if necessary, by fomenting a Palestinian civil war. At a recent meeting of the international diplomatic "Quartet," [a group made up of the United States, the European Union, the United Nations, and Russia] General Keith Dayton, the American security envoy, pitched the idea of building up a "Special Presidential Guard" around Abbas to crush Hamas militias in house-to-house fighting. European diplomats at the meeting were appalled, but the Americans are reported to have already begun assembling the force.

Bush's moves to block a return to the peace table accelerated in September [2006] after Palestinian negotiators reached a breakthrough in talks on forming a national unity government. At the risk of alienating hardline elements in his own party, Prime Minister Haniyeh decided to accept the 2002 Arab League peace plan—which calls for full peace and normalization of relations with Israel in exchange for a withdrawal to the 1967 borders—the diplomatic stance for the new joint government.

Haniyeh was encouraged by signs that key European leaders were willing to resume contacts with a Palestinian government that embraced the formula. But within days, Bush held a White House meeting with Abbas' advisors to warn that the Arab League plan is "not enough" and that Washington would refuse cooperation with a government formed on those terms.

Desperate for U.S. support, Abbas backtracked, insisting publicly that Hamas accept Bush's three conditions in order for a
unity government to go forward.

Since then, the political initiative has returned to the more
hardline elements in Hamas led by Damascus-based exile
leader Khaled Meshaal. Locked in a rivalry with the increasingly popular prime minister, Meshaal has signaled his interest
in government technocrats chosen jointly by Fatah and Hamas [the 2 Palestinian parties], which would have the effect of
sidelining Haniyeh. . . .

But once again, the decision rests with President Bush. No
deal will go forward without guarantees that the international
siege will be lifted. With Democrats in full support of Bush's
Mideast policy and Europeans unable to influence Washington, the stalemate could degenerate until the conflict explodes
yet again.

Israel Plans to Keep the Occupied Territories Because of Their Vital Water Resources

Isabelle Humphries

Isabelle Humphries is conducting PhD research on the Palestinian refugee community inside Israel's 1948 borders.

In months when Israel is not pounding the life out of its Lebanese neighbors, a tourist to Israel may hire a car and drive around the beautiful northern regions of former mandate Palestine and Syria. Here one may look around at the stunningly green surroundings, go kayaking in the Jordan River, admire the beautiful waterfalls at ancient Banyas [spas] in the Golan [one of the territories occupied by Israel], or dip one's feet in the waters of the Sea of Galilee. Those feeling adventurous may hand over their passports at the gate, enter the Israeli-occupied Alawite [Islamic] village of Ghajar, and look down at the little stream of the Wazzani in the small valley below.

Water Is the Root of Israeli-Palestinian Conflict

Israel has not ensconced itself in the Golan Heights for mere tourism opportunities, however. The Israeli media machine would have one believe that the country is engaged in a struggle to protect its very existence against imaginary Arab military giants. Yet a trip around the places in which it chooses to maintain its borders is far more revealing of the root of conflict with its Arab neighbors—water. Israel has no plans to make peace with Syria and return the Golan Heights, because

Isabelle Humphries, "Breaching Borders: The Role of Water in the Middle East Conflict," *Washington Report on Middle East Affairs*, vol. 25, September–October 2006, pp. 20–21. Copyright 2006 American Educational Trust. All rights reserved. Reproduced by permission.

by doing so it would give up its control of springs, rivers and the Sea of Galilee. Nor will it hand over any significant West Bank [an Israeli-occupied territory] land to Palestinians, for in doing so Israel would have to abandon lush aquifers (underground water reserves), key access to the Dead Sea, the Jordan River, and surrounding fertile plains.

Even where Palestinians remain in control of small pieces of land, Israeli water policy usually sees to it that there is not enough water to grow crops.

Division and distribution of a static resource such as land is difficult enough, but problems are magnified when the resource is able to flow across international boundaries. Take the Israeli furor over Lebanon's installation of new pumping facilities on the Wazzani River in the fall of 2002. Despite the fact that the activity took place entirely on Lebanese land, Israel raised a ruckus because the Wazzani is a key tributary of the Hasbani River. And although the Hasbani flows for 25 miles inside Lebanon, it crosses into the Israeli-occupied Syrian Golan, feeding into the Banias and Dan Rivers, which in turn flow into the Jordan—ultimately providing water to the rapidly reducing Sea of Galilee, Israel's largest source of fresh water.

While Beirut stated that it was Lebanon's internationally recognized right to pump Wazzani waters for surrounding low-income Shi'i villages, Israel objected, claiming, as usual, that the "terrorist" entities of Syria and Hezbollah were behind the development plan. Lebanon retorted by pointing out that even after pump installation, it would be taking only 10 million cubic meters annually—while Israel, on the other hand, uses some 150 million cubic meters a year from the Wazzani and Hasbani.

That particular episode of the water conflict did not erupt into full-scale war, but at other times water has provided the trigger. In his memoirs, [former Israeli prime minister] Ariel Sharon claimed that the 1967 war (resulting in Israeli occupation of the Golan and prevention of Syrian access to the Sea of Galilee) was launched as an unavoidable response to Syrian attempts three years earlier to divert the headwaters of the Jordan.

The Historical Evidence

An analysis of historical evidence, however, provides a very different story of the events leading to the 1967 war. It was Israel, in fact, which first made moves to divert the headwaters, provoking an international crisis, yet convincing many that Syria was the aggressor. Israeli historian Avi Shlaim dates Israel's first attempt to divert the Jordan River to as early as 1953, when Syria responded not by attacking the Jewish state, but complaining to the U.N., which eventually put a halt to the Israeli plan the following year. Ten years later however, Israel began to pump water from the Sea of Galilee into its National Water Carrier—a grave threat to vital Syrian, Lebanese and Jordanian water sources. It was in response to this Israeli move that Syria planned to divert Jordan water into its own territory.

Remaining in control of the Golan Heights today allows Israel to irrigate settlements as far as the Negev desert through its National Water Carrier pipeline. The diversion of waters to this artificial carrier has grave implications, resulting in the depletion and salinization of the Jordan River south of the Sea of Galilee, and devastating agriculture on the Jordanian side of the river. The Jordanian government's diversion of the Yarmuk [River] cannot adequately compensate for this loss.

Israeli Water Policies and the Palestinians

Israeli control of water is as much of a concern for Palestinians as it is for Arab neighbors. Whether for the few Palestinian farmers remaining inside the Israeli state, or those in the

West Bank and Gaza, Israeli water policy is directed at destroying any remaining Palestinian agriculture. The million Palestinians inside Israel are primarily a flexible manual labor force for Jewish industry, as are—when curfews allow—1967 Palestinians. Even where Palestinians remain in control of small pieces of land, Israeli water policy usually sees to it that there is not enough water to grow crops.

International law clearly states that Israel should not be taking water from areas occupied in 1967.

Situated above the mountain aquifer, central West Bank towns such as Qalqilya and Nablus have traditionally exported crops across the Middle East. Yet today, despite the availability of sophisticated technology, Israeli policy means that many Palestinians do not have enough water even for themselves, let alone to irrigate the few fields that have not yet been confiscated.

Palestinians should have ready access to water from the mountain aquifer, the Jordan River basin and the Gazan coastal aquifer. Aquifers are replenished through rainwater seeping through the ground, and water accessible via wells and springs. According to Oslo [peace proposals negotiated in Oslo, Norway, in 1993], two West Bank aquifers are to be shared between Israelis and Palestinians, leaving the Gazan coastal and the third West Bank aquifer solely to Palestinians. (Palestinians, of course, have no access to the Sea of Galilee—their share having been taken in 1948). According to Oslo, Syrians, Jordanians, Palestinians and Israelis all have a share in the Jordan River system (although 97 percent of the river passes through areas only occupied by Israel since 1967). Currently Israel has assured that its citizens have the highest per capita water consumption in the entire Middle East—and four times as much as the Palestinians among whom they live.

Israel's Illegal Use of Regional Water

International law clearly states that Israel should not be taking water from areas occupied in 1967. Yet even if Oslo had been followed to the letter, it assured inequality by giving Israeli water authorities overall control of water resources. Palestinians may not drill for water without Israeli approval, yet Israel can pump as much water as it likes into its illegal settlements. More than 80 percent of West Bank water is taken by Israelis on both sides of the 1967 line.

What is certain is that there will be no long-term security for any resident of the Middle East without . . . a just solution to the sharing of water resources.

Israeli occupation has prevented the development of a Palestinian water infrastructure which would make maximum use of the minimum resources. Some 200,000 West Bankers do not even have access to piped water systems, while the settlements around them are kept green with lawn sprinklers. Palestinians living under occupation are forced to rely on expensive private water tankers, which of course cannot reach them in times of closure. Ironically, some of the water is bought directly from Israelis at inflated prices, despite the fact that the water originates in the West Bank.

In contravention of Oslo, Israel continues to pump from the Gaza coastal aquifer—which, as levels fall dangerously low, draws in salt water from the Mediterranean. Two-thirds of water is used for the Israeli agricultural sector, which represents only 3 percent of Israel's annual GDP [gross domestic product], while the greater percentage of Palestinian farmers must rely on insufficient sources of rainwater for 90 percent of their agricultural activity. Desperate for water, Gazans also are overpumping this source, as their inadequate sewage networks continue to leak raw sewage into the supply. Medical sources in Gaza note an increase in kidney disease and other dangerous water-related illnesses. The U.N. estimates that in less than 15 years Gazans will not have access to drinkable water.

What little Palestinian water infrastructure there is falls regular victim to Israeli military assault. From the destruction of 140 wells in the 1967 war, to soldiers sniping at water tanks on family homes, to settlers vandalizing and polluting water-courses, to confiscation of wells for the building of "security" walls, Palestinians have no chance to improve their situation. . . .

What is certain is that there will be no long-term security for any resident of the Middle East without fair distribution and a just solution to the sharing of water resources. Without regional cooperation on protecting rapidly depleting resources such as the Jordan River and the Dead Sea, not even Israel can count on secure water forever.

Foreign Interests Do Not Want the Arab-Israeli Conflict to Be Resolved

Joel Bainerman

Joel Bainerman, who immigrated to Israel in 1983, lectures and writes about Israeli and Middle East economic and political subjects. He is also the author of The Crimes of a President, *a 1992 book that documents the covert side of American-Israel bilateral relations.*

For more than 75 years, western diplomats have been coming up with peace initiatives to solve the Arab Israeli conflict. Yet they always fail. Why? What keeps the Middle East conflict going?

If we are going to devise a solution, we must first understand why the conflict continues to exist. To do this, we have to view the situation from the top down, rather than from the bottom up. This is completely opposite to the way most Jews and Arabs have been conditioned to look at the situation. Jews focus on the damage Arabs/Palestinians cause, and believe that damage to be the cause of the conflict, when it is really only a result of it. They view the conflict and its origins from the bottom up. Arabs/Palestinians concentrate on the damage Israel causes and believe this to be the cause of the conflict, when it is really only a result of it. They too relate to the situation from the bottom up.

Five Factors Are Key

To understand what really causes the Middle East conflict to continue, one must look at the issue from the top down. To get a more accurate picture of what lies behind the continued existence of the conflict, let's acknowledge these five factors, which serve to perpetuate rather than solve the problem:

1. *The vested interests of the Foreign Elite (FE)*: There is a third entity in the conflict in addition to the Israelis and the Arabs: the foreigners (in order of importance, the US, Britain, Russia, China, France, Germany). Without them, there would be no Middle East conflict because it is the foreign influence that keeps the situation from being resolved. Unfortunately, both Palestinian Arabs and Israeli Jews believe they are each other's worst enemy without considering the third element: the foreigners that [are] the enemy of both. The thing that Arabs and Jews have most in common is this common enemy, yet the leaders on both sides (not being legitimate or independent) tell their people that the other side is their number one enemy. Hence the conflict continues.

2. *Control of Middle East oil*: The foreigners interfere in the Arab-Israeli conflict in order to exploit and control the vast petroleum resources in the region. If there were no oil, there would be no petrodollars to recycle; the foreigners would have no reason to dominate the region.

3. *Weapons sales*: If there were a worldwide ban on arms sales to the Middle East, there would be no more radical Arab dictators with modern arms. If the foreigners stopped selling advanced weaponry to nations of the Middle East, the conflict would end.

4. *The mainstream media*: If the mainstream media in the West stopped reporting on the "search for peace in the Middle East", peace would prevail. By keeping the region's unstable image alive, the media, as the sole source of information by which people can formulate their perceptions, provide an excuse for the foreigners to interfere, and at the same time serve to convince everyone that these western nations want peace, despite the

fact that they have been seeking it for over 50 years, in vain. The media never question the intentions or agendas of the FE. The media thus provide the glue which keeps the conflict going. Without the mainstream media constantly reporting on the conflict, there would be peace, as everyone would forget that the Middle East is unstable and thus in need of stabilizing via new peace initiatives.

5. *Corrupt national leadership of Middle East nations*: It isn't peace between Arabs and Jews that interests the FE, but rather the continuation of the conflict. The way they do that is by corrupting/controlling the national leaders of both sides. The reason why legitimate, popular leaders are not at the helms of countries in the Middle East is because the FE will topple any leader who doesn't cater to their desires before the needs of their own people. If Middle East leaders are selected and deemed popular by their own people, the FE will demonize them as radicals/extremists, terrorist leaders or enemies of peace, and thus de-legitimize them in the world arena. How can genuine co-existence take hold if the leaders of both sides are more interested in pleasing their foreign masters than their own peoples?

The goal of the "Foreign Elite" is to keep the oil flowing to western economies at a relatively low price.

Unless these five basic factors are understood, the true causes that extend the conflict will never be understood. Instead, each side will go on blaming the other, seeking to take the high moral ground and convince their own people and those from abroad that they are right and the other side is wrong. This will lead only to more death and destruction. The technique is called divide and rule, and it has been a favorite of the FE for decades. . . .

Why the Middle East Conflict
Never Gets Solved

Everyone in the world is morally bound up with the Arab-Israeli conflict. Yet can it be possible that the entire conflict is based on the lack of morality of one side or the other? Can all that has happened in the region over the past half century be the result of one people not behaving nicely toward the other? What other regional conflicts are defined in this way? What other regional conflicts continue for more than a half a century, look like they are finally being solved, and then come roaring back in the way the Middle East conflict has?

Let's think for a moment, and ask: Do regional wars and conflicts continue for seven decades because one side isn't acting nicely toward the other? Is the conflict's existence merely due to the actions of each or both sides—the 5 million Jews and the 4 million Arabs—who simply don't like each other?

Can that really be the answer? That is certainly the way the mainstream press and the academic world present it. Oil and arms sales are never part of the explanation. How could so many newspapers and TV stations miss out on this side of the region's affairs and focus solely on "new peace initiatives"?

One could argue, with justification, that the Israelis are not acting nicely toward the Palestinians—that they oppress them, restrict their movements, blow up their houses, etc. But that alone still doesn't account for the continuation of the conflict. The Israelis are right when they argue that the Palestinian Authority is corrupt and the Palestinian leadership hasn't done enough to crack down on terrorism, but that too doesn't explain why this 75-year-old conflict is still with us.

While it may even be true that the Arabs don't recognize Israel's right to exist, Israel doesn't stop existing because of that. The refusal of the Arabs to recognize Israel's existence is not the reason why the Middle East still festers.

So why has this conflict been going on for nearly a century? Not only does the Middle East conflict continue to exist, it actually gets worse decade after decade. What other regional conflict actually looks like it is being solved, and then, 10 years later, returns to a state much worse than before? . . .

The Function of Oil, Weapons, and the US Dollar in the Middle East Conflict

There is a view in the mainstream media that assumes the only concern the western nations have in the Middle East is for Arabs and Jews to kiss and make up. Yet after all their years of being involved in peace-making, how come there isn't any peace?

Because peace is not good business for the "Foreign Elite". What is important is maintaining the supremacy of the US dollar in world markets, recycling petrodollars to earn profits from the oil industry, and the sale of military products to the oil-rich Arab regimes. The unwritten agreement that the US has with the rulers of the oil states is that the oil will be priced in US dollars, and in return the US will protect them. While *Fox, Time* and *CNN* never discuss this issue, it is imperative for the strength of the US dollar that oil is only in US currency.

When oil is sold in US dollars, countries around the world need to maintain a certain level of US currency in the reserves of their central bank to finance their oil purchases. OPEC [Oil Producing and Exporting Countries], is a cartel created by the US specifically for this purpose. At the end of 2000, the Bank for International Settlements estimates world dollar reserves of $1.45 trillion, or 76% of the total world reserves of $1.09 trillion. If oil was priced in other currencies, most countries would have little need to stockpile dollars, and thus all the currency the US government has printed over the years would be of value only in the US. This would flood the country with dollars and cause huge inflation. In addition, current and future trade and current account deficits would no longer be financed by the foreigners who purchase American Treasury bills and other US-dominated debt instruments. In other words, the US would no longer be an economic superpower.

In a brilliant essay on this subject entitled "A Macroeconomic and Geostrategic Analysis of the Unspoken Truth," economist William Clark wrote in January 2003: "The Federal Reserve's greatest nightmare is that OPEC will switch from a dollar standard to a euro standard." Iraq actually made this switch. The real reason the [George W.] Bush administration wants a puppet government in Iraq, or more importantly, the reason why the corporate-military-industrial network wants a puppet government in Iraq is so that it will revert back to a dollar standard. . . .

The goal of the "Foreign Elite" is to keep the oil flowing to western economies at a relatively low price so as not to harm the profits the elite oil companies earn from refining and marketing petroleum products, and ensuring that this oil remains priced in US dollars. To do that, foreigners have to prop up undemocratic and corrupt regimes (i.e., Saudi Arabia, Kuwait, United Arab Emirates, Oman, Qatar and Bahrain) so they will continue to serve foreign interests. In return, these countries keep the price of oil relatively low, keep the oil priced in US dollars, and never move upstream in the petroleum production process so as to compete with foreign oil companies.

Is it merely a coincidence that there is vast oil reserves in the Middle East, while at the same time the region is home to a seven-decade-long conflict?

Recycling Petrodollars

The other unwritten law is that a certain amount of the oil revenues earned by the oil-rich states must be spent on the purchase of weapons. In 2002, Arab governments in the Middle East spent $52 billion on their military forces, of which $18 billion was for purchases from foreign countries. Arab countries devote 8%–11% of their national incomes to defense (23% of all government expenditures). In the past decade, Saudi Arabia alone has spent over $100 billion on weapons.

According to the Federation of American Scientists [a group that promotes humanitarian uses of science and technology], in the decade after the Gulf War (1991–2001) the US sold more than $43 billion worth of weapons, equipment and military construction projects to Saudi Arabia, and $16 billion more to Kuwait, Qatar, Bahrain and the United Arab Emirates. Saudi Arabia alone imports about $15 billion worth of weapons each year. Instead of using this wealth for building an economic infrastructure throughout the region, it is wasted on arms. The rest of the oil revenues (after basic government expenditures are met) are deposited in western banks as the private property of the corrupted Arab leaders. This benefits both the leaders and the large western banking interests.

This process is called recycling petrodollars. As much of that wealth winds up in banks controlled by the foreign elite, this is another way that foreigners profit from the continued tension in the Middle East. Another activity of the foreigners is to sell massive amounts of military hardware and technology to Arab dictators like Saddam Hussein and then, years later, when the dictator doesn't do what the foreigners want, the dictator becomes a threat to regional stability and an expensive (to the public at large, not to the arms industry) military invasion is suddenly required to contain him. When the smoke clears, nobody points a finger at the foreigners, accusing them of arming the dictator in the first place.

As no Arab country has a military industry, all weapons in the region are imported. If the western nations were truly interested in bringing peace to the Middle East, they would have placed a moratorium on arms sales to the region decades ago. Instead, they sell tens of billions worth of military hardware every year to the unstable regimes of the region. So the entities that are sending special envoys to "help the two sides make peace" are at the same time the main providers of weapons to the region. Somehow, this contradiction is never exposed.

This is where the Palestinian-Israeli conflict serves its purpose. Keeping the conflict alive means a never-ending moral crusade can be carried out by both Arabs and Jews, each blaming the other for keeping the conflict festering, each pointing fingers at the other side rather than at the foreigners. Is it merely a coincidence that there is vast oil reserves in the Middle East, while at the same time the region is home to a seven-decade-long conflict? If there were no oil, would there have been an Arab-Israeli conflict? As long as the Arabs and Jews are blaming each other, the foreigners' role will go unnoticed—as will their profits.

CHAPTER 4

Should the United States Be Involved with the Problems of the Middle East?

Chapter Preface

Throughout its history, the Middle East has been dominated by powerful outside forces. For many centuries, the area was under the control of the Ottoman Empire, a Turkish power, and after World War I the region was ruled by Great Britain. Since World War II, however, the United States has been the dominant power in the Middle East. Historians agree that U.S. policies in the region have been directed primarily toward advancing U.S. interests—most especially access to the region's vast reserves of oil. Protecting this vital U.S. interest is likely an underlying reason for numerous American interventions, including the 2003 U.S.-led invasion of Iraq. This U.S. strategy, however, may have come at a huge cost—a wave of anti-American sentiment and terrorism that is sweeping the globe.

One of the first Mideast policies developed by the United States, for example, was its strong support for the nation of Israel, a nation created in 1948 in the Middle East to provide a home for Jews who had been persecuted in Germany and other parts of Europe. Although begun primarily as a humanitarian policy, the U.S. pro-Israel policy evolved into one designed to turn Israel into a proxy, or representative, for U.S. power in the Middle East. In return for supporting Israel both politically and militarily, Israel over the years has acted as a local U.S. ally helping to maintain regional stability. Because Israel has historically been seen by surrounding Arab countries as an interloper on Arab lands, however, U.S. support for Israel also has caused widespread anti-American sentiment among Arabs in the Middle East.

An example of the Israeli-U.S. alliance can be seen in America's intervention in a civil war that broke out in Lebanon in 1975. The United States provided military and other support for a June 1982 invasion of Lebanon by Israel to root out Palestinian militias who were using Lebanon as a base to launch attacks into Israeli areas. U.S. officials brokered a deal that provided for Palestinian forces to withdraw from Lebanon and for the appointment of a new Lebanese government that would be an ally of the United States. U.S. troops later were stationed in Beirut, Lebanon's capital, to protect this new government, but they soon became the targets of a 1983 suicide bomb attack that killed nearly three hundred Americans and led to a U.S. withdrawal in early 1984. Since then, Lebanon has become a center of anti-American resentment and home to Hezbollah, an Iran-backed, radical Islamist group.

Other U.S. involvements in the Middle East occurred as part of the Cold War—the long rivalry between America and the Soviet Union that arose after World War II. During this period, the United States sought to prevent the Soviets from gaining a foothold in the region because such Soviet involvement might have threatened America's newly established oil concessions in Saudi Arabia and its interests in other oil-producing countries.

One of these Cold War crises, for example, occurred in Iran when the government of prime minister Mohammed Mossadegh nationalized (or converted to government ownership) a British oil company that earlier had negotiated an oil deal with the country. Britain and the United States responded by imposing economic sanctions on Iran, and this in turn, led to widespread political unrest. In 1953, fearing that this instability could result in a Soviet takeover, the United States organized a military coup to oust the elected prime minister and return the exiled Iranian shah (or king) to power. With full American support, the shah of Iran (Mohammad Reza Shah Pahlavi) then ruled Iran for the next twenty-six years using brutally repressive and undemocratic methods. Iran, like Israel, became an American proxy. However, the shah was finally overthrown in 1979 in an anti-American, Islamic revolution. Islamists still rule Iran today and over the years have supported a number of anti-American terrorist groups such as Hezbollah in Lebanon, Hamas in Palestine, and, many believe, a number of the insurgent groups now fighting in Iraq. Many commentators also believe that Iran's efforts to develop nuclear weapons is part of a challenge to U.S. dominance in the Middle East.

Another well-known U.S. Mideast intervention was the United States' support for Iraq during the 1980–1990 Iran-Iraq War. Because U.S. officials wanted to prevent the new Islamic government in Iran from gaining power and destabilizing the oil-rich region, the United States provided large amounts of military and technological support to Iraqi dictator Saddam Hussein, even though his regime was previously listed as one that supported terrorist groups. Among the items given Iraq was anthrax (a microbe used to make biological weapons) and toxic chemicals (used to make chemical weapons). U.S. officials then looked the other way when Saddam used these weapons on the Iranians and even inside Iraq on his own people.

This U.S. support for Saddam Hussein later came back to haunt the United States, when Saddam, emboldened by earlier U.S. support, invaded Kuwait in 1990 in a blatant bid to take over some of its rich oil fields. This led to the first Gulf War, in 1991, in which U.S. forces were sent to the region to remove Iraqi troops from Kuwait. Thereafter, the United States was instrumental in getting the United Nations (UN) to authorize economic sanctions that crippled Iraq and impoverished its population for the next decade. After the war, American troops were stationed in nearby Saudi Arabia, but this continuing U.S. presence, along with the sanctions on Iraq, helped to inspire radical, anti-American terrorists, including Osama bin Laden, the leader of al Qaeda, the group responsible for the 9/11 terrorist attacks. And of course that attack led not only to a U.S. attack on Afghanistan, an al Qaeda sanctuary, but also to today's ongoing war in Iraq.

Although U.S. policies, in large part, have been successful at keeping oil flowing to America and its allies, U.S. involvement in the Middle East is viewed very negatively by many people in the region. Many local inhabitants see America as a nation that has helped Israel to repress Palestinians' desires for an independent nation, supported corrupt Arab leaders who do not act in the best interests of their people, and imposed U.S. interests instead of letting countries in the region determine their own fates. The viewpoints in this chapter address this vital question of America's role in the Middle East.

The Vital Interests of the United States Are at Stake in the Middle East

Doug Edelman

Doug Edelman is a conservative political commentator and a contributing editor for the Conservative Voice, *an online publication.*

When one hears the words "Middle East", most people form an immediate image in their minds: Sand, Oil, AK-47's and explosions. The region has been a hotbed of warfare and terror for generations.

Because the US is still heavily dependent upon foreign oil, our national interests are at stake in the region. For this reason, every administration since [Harry] Truman has had to address Mid-East issues as a significant segment of American foreign policy.

Unfortunately, Americans in general—and our politicians in particular—don't seem to "get it" when it comes to the nature of the situation in the region. This fundamental disconnect with the realities of the region dooms every effort and initiative put forth out of Washington to failure.

The Enemy

We are currently at war—but we don't seem to know with whom or with what! The so-called "War on Terror" is a misnomer. Terror is a tactic, not an enemy. We are at war with those who utilize this tactic against us, our interests and our allies. This enemy is not bound by geography or political borders. This enemy does not wear a uniform. This enemy recruits women and children into warfare. The enemy is an ideology! The ideology is Jihad [holy war]. Islamic radicalism.

There will never be an end to Islamic effort[s] to re-take the Holy Land and to drive the Jews into the sea.

Jihadists have only one goal—to establish the world-wide caliphate. To institute Sharia [Muslim religious] law on a global scale. To convert or kill any non-Muslim. They are willing and eager to die in this pursuit. Jihad is not localized to Iraq/ Afghanistan. It is not restricted to the Arab/Israeli conflict. It is global in scope and in intent.

The Arab/Israeli Conflict

From the moment Israel was formed as a nation, the surrounding Islamic states have sought her destruction. They view the Jewish State as an affront, akin to pigs and monkeys trampling their holy land. This offense extends beyond the jihadist ideology, which seeks global caliphate. It permeates all Islam. There will never be an end to Islamic effort[s] to re-take the Holy Land and to drive the Jews into the sea. Peaceful co-existence is not a long-term option for most of Islam— much less for the Jihadis.

The "we must understand why they hate us" crowd loves to point to US support for Israel as the cause of all our troubles with the Jihadis. If only we'd hang Israel out to dry, they'd leave us alone. But the Islamic Radicals are not only seeking to destroy Israel. And they don't hate us only because of our support for Israel . . . though it is a great rhetorical tool for them to recruit soldiers to their cause. No, the jihadis hate the US for much more than our support of Israel. They hate us for our democracy. They hate us for our wealth. They hate us for our liberation of women. They hate us for our freedom. They hate us for our immoralities. Most of all they hate us for our being "infidels" and having influence in the world. If Israel did not exist, we would still be their target and focus.

Dipomacy/Negotiation

The West is obsessed with talk. Political correctness demands that everything be negotiated and worked out across the table. Perhaps this is desirable amongst the nations of polite society ... however, negotiation is by definition the art of compromise. The finding of a middle ground which can be mutually acceptable. Unfortunately, for the jihadis there is no acceptable middle ground. Convert or kill all infidels, or die trying, is their only option. They will, however, use our obsession with negotiation to their own advantage. Placating us with talk, they gain opportunity to regroup, rearm, and strategize their next attack. Witness the result of Israel's giveaway of Gaza!

Diplomacy is only possible where both sides are capable of compromise. When one party to a negotiation has an immutable agenda and the willingness to die in the pursuit of its fulfillment, there is nothing to be gained by negotiation as there is no possibility of mitigating their position. There is no mutually beneficial or mutually acceptable common ground. To believe otherwise is little more than politically correct pie-in-the-sky pipe dreaming.

Democratization/Nation Building

Americans believe that by democratizing Iraq and Afghanistan we will create allies friendly to the West. By liberating these peoples from dictatorial regimes and creating new democratic political entities we are supposed to reap the benefit of the appreciation and friendship of the people.

While on a local level, we are seeing some encouraging results, towns and villages are showing friendliness to our troops as they build schools and hospitals and rebuild infrastructure; however the overall effort is unlikely to result in a sustained pro-western culture. A political democracy does not inherently create a pro-western mindset. Witness the recent election victories of Hamas [a militant Palestinian group]! When given the vote, the choice went for the terrorists!

Vigilance Is the Key

Is there a workable solution? One must wonder. The apocalyptic minded among us will point out that the conflict is predicted to go on right to the very end. The pragmatic will recognize that maintaining a long-term presence in Iraq/Afghanistan would be considered an occupation, which is an inflammatory provocation. Conversely, a precipitous withdrawal projects weakness and leaves a vacuum. Political Correctness will keep us from leveling hotspots like Fallujah [an insurgent stronghold in Iraq]. It will prevent us from implementing prudent profiling. There will be inside-the-US attacks—it is an inevitability.

Reducing our dependence on Middle Eastern oil will help—both in terms of the blackmail threat they hold over us with the oil, and in reducing our funding of these states.

We must acknowledge that Saudi Arabia is no friend of the US as long as they support the madrassas [Muslim schools] which preach hate and train children to be jihadis. The house of Saud may occasionally keep a lid on oil prices—but this alone does not make them our ally.

Long-term occupation by ground troops has been shown to be ineffective given the impatient and risk averse nature of our present-day society. Therefore a strategic shift to an over-the-horizon force to represent America's interests may become the next movie. When things heat up to a threat against our interests, a few cruise missiles or daisy-cutters will make our point for us. Rapid response of this nature to belligerent acts against us may prove at least as effective as long-term occupation has been.

The reality of life today is that we must be ever vigilant against Jihad, at home and abroad. The threat is not just "over there" but in our own neighborhoods; and it's not going away any time soon—regardless of who holds elected office or of their policies. Whether we choose to acknowledge it or not, we are engaged in a cultural duel to the death. We had best take stock and develop a strategy to survive.

Only the United States Can Broker Peace Between Israel and the Palestinians

Stephen D. Hayes

Stephen D. Hayes is a writer with a twenty-five-year background of working in the U.S. government.

The Palestinian-Israeli conflict has now been waged for more than half a century. In fact, depending on one's reading of events in the region in the late 1800s and early 1900s, it can be argued that the struggle has gone on for more than a hundred years. The problem seems intractable, with a solution always just beyond reach.

But a solution is unlikely to be found by the parties themselves because of their internal divisions and weak leadership. Only the United States has both the requisite influence over Israel and the ability to move the Palestinians toward a lasting settlement. . . .

Through a Palestinian Lens

Given our leadership role in the world and in the Middle East, we Americans have a special responsibility to understand the history of the region, the origins of the conflict *and* the perspectives of peoples on both sides. . . . The perspective of the Palestinians . . . is the piece of the puzzle least understood by the American public. We don't have to like it. We don't have to agree with all of it. But if we are going to be productively engaged in that part of the world, we had better fully understand it.

The average American thinks of Israel as a small, heroic nation that has been under almost constant siege by hostile

Arab neighbors. We tend to view Israel as a peace-loving democracy that has usually been the aggrieved party in this conflict. While focusing on the historic tragedy of the Jewish people, [we] have too often ignored or misunderstood the Palestinian perspective, which is no less important.

The claim that Palestine was a "land without a people" was false.

To see Palestine and Israel the way the Palestinians do, one must start at the beginning . . . before the establishment of the State of Israel, before World War II . . . before World War I. During the latter years of the 19th century, Jewish leaders in Europe began thinking and writing and organizing around the concept of a "homeland" for the Jewish people. In 1901, one of those leaders, Israel Zwangwill, published *The Return to Palestine* and described the designated territory as "A land without a people for a people without land." This catchy phrase—implying that Palestine was unpopulated and available for the taking—became a popular rallying cry for the Zionist movement [the name of the Jewish "return to Israel" movement].

The claim that Palestine was a "land without a people" was false. Population estimates prior to 1900 are not precise. But it is fairly well documented that by the mid-1800s, there were several hundred thousand people living in "the Holy Land", or Palestine, of which less than 7% were Jews. A British post–World War I census, conducted in 1922, showed a population (in the area that is now roughly modern day Israel and the occupied territories of the West Bank and Gaza) of more than 750,000 consisting of the following: Jews—83,790; Christians—71,464; Muslims—598,177.

Palestine was therefore hardly a "land without a people" since the overwhelming majority of the Christians were Arabs and almost 90% of the total population was Arab. So it is critical to understand, that as Palestinian Arabs look back at their own recent history they see a Palestine where Jews, Muslims and Christians all lived, but where Muslims were the overwhelming majority.

Jewish Immigration

Between 1905 and 1935, more than 230,000 Jews moved into Palestine from Europe, Russia and other parts of the world. . . . The rise of Nazism [the political ideology promoted by Adolf Hitler, the leader of Germany] and the increasingly desperate situation of the Jews in the 1930s and 1940s propelled this wave of immigration. But the Palestinians had no involvement in the gathering storm in Europe and saw the massive influx of Jews as unwarranted and unwanted.

Through the eyes of a Palestinian Arab, . . . the creation of Israel was and continues to be regarded as a gross injustice.

In the mid-1930s, Palestinian Arabs urged Britain, which controlled Palestine, to stop the Jewish immigration. Instead, Britain increased authorized immigration by 10% and the Jewish population grew to 300,000. Yet despite the heavy foreign influx of Jews, they were still less than 25% of the total population. And as late as 1948, only 6.6% of the land in Palestine was owned by Jews. As the number of immigrants grew, tensions and conflicts understandably rose. The arrival of additional immigrants continued through the 1930's, swelling with the rise of the Nazi era in Germany, into the 1940's and during and after World War II. In the immediate aftermath of the Second World War with it's ghastly saga of the Holocaust [Hitler's program of exterminating Jews and some other groups], the stream of Jewish immigrants to Palestine was seen by most of the outside world as a just and deserving reward for a downtrodden and persecuted people. But in the eyes of the Palestinians, who had little knowledge of and no responsibility for Nazism, rising Jewish immigration was a virtual invasion by outsiders of their land, homes, villages and towns.

The Birth of Israel

International support for the Zionists was based on the Balfour declaration issued by the United Kingdom in 1917 and that was later incorporated into the Versailles Peace Treaty [the treaty that ended World War I]. The Balfour declaration called for a "homeland" for the Jewish people. But a much ignored passage of the text also stated that "nothing shall be done which may prejudice the civil and religious rights of existing non-Jewish communities living in Palestine." Palestinian Arabs fought the imposition of a Jewish colony in the midst of their own homeland, where they were a clear majority. For years, they took solace in believing that their "rights" would be protected. But this promise was violated, since until the very end of the British era, London favored the interests of the Zionists at the expense of the Palestinians.

As a nation, Israel was born from bloody conflict. Ze'ev Jabotinsky, one of the early leaders of the right wing of the Zionist movement, said, "(The) only way to liberate the country (that is, Palestine) is by the sword." And indeed, modern Israeli historians have confirmed that hundreds of thousands of Palestinians were forcibly removed from what they regarded as their historic homeland, or fled in fear of their lives. Through the eyes of a Palestinian Arab, then, the creation of Israel was and continues to be regarded as a gross injustice.

The 1967 War

With this history as a backdrop, it is not difficult to see why Palestinians and other Arabs view the fighting throughout the 1940s and 1950s, the Six-Day War of June 1967, the 1973 Yom Kippur War and all the subsequent conflicts as honorable struggles to redress this injustice.

The aftermath of one of those wars, in June 1967, deepened the conflict. As a result of their smashing military victory, Israel took control of even more land, including Gaza and the West Bank. Historians differ on whether Israel or the Arabs were responsible for not making peace after 1967, but Palestinians regarded this as another grave injustice.

In the early decades of the Israeli-Palestinian struggle, Israeli leaders, seeking to justify their national claim to all of Palestine, worked to deny the legitimacy of Palestinian claims and even Palestinians' identity as a people. Former Israeli Prime Minister Golda Meir famously remarked in 1969 that, "It was not as though there was a Palestinian people. . . . They did not exist." It was not until the beginning of the issuance of the Oslo Declaration of Principles in 1993 that Israel formally acknowledged the PLO [Palestine Liberation Organization] and the Palestinian national movement and that [that] would require reconciling their respective claims for the land they shared.

Although most, but not all, Palestinian leaders now recognize the need for a territorial compromise and a two-state peace based on the creation of a Palestinian state in the territories occupied in 1967, all Palestinians continue to see themselves as victims of a long and severe military occupation and conquest by Israel. Although they are prepared to make peace with Israel, they have not abandoned their historic narrative that Zionism has been both morally and legally wrong, and that they, rather than Israel, are the primary victims of the conflict. Most Israelis, in contrast, continue to see themselves, based on their historic and religious ties to the land of Palestine and Palestinian violence and terrorism, as the primary victim. . . .

U.S. Interests

America's interests in the region are essentially four:

1. We have a long-standing alliance with Israel, and it is in our interest that we are, in fact, and perceived as, a reli-

able friend and ally. Therefore, it is not only in our interest but is consistent with our values to continue to act to preserve Israel as a secure and viable nation.

2. At the same time, it is also in our interest to be, and to be seen as, consistently supporting the core American values of freedom and self-determination for peoples all over the world, including the Palestinians. If we are supporting the Jews' right to independence and a homeland, we cannot without severe inconsistency, fail to support the realization of the same rights for the Palestinians. This is U.S. official policy as reflected in President [George W.] Bush's explicit call for a two-state solution and an independent Palestinian state.

3. There has developed a deep hostility toward the U.S. in the Arab/Muslim world over America's perceived failure to work in an even-handed fashion for peace. But the U.S. has vital economic interests in the Arab and Muslim worlds. The world's 1.2 billion Muslims represent an important market for American goods and services. A significant portion of our vital oil and gas imports originates in Arab/Muslim countries. By contrast, with a total population less than 7 million and no significant natural resources, Israel holds relatively modest economic or commercial value for the [United States.]

4. Finally, the U.S. obviously has a paramount interest in quelling international terrorism. The ongoing Israeli occupation of Palestinian land is viewed throughout the Muslim world as a gross injustice and that sense of injustice continues to be an effective recruiting tool and motivator for the terrorist networks. Therefore, forging an equitable, American-led peace would help combat terrorism.

Israeli Interests

Israeli interests in all this are at the same time simpler and more complex. Israel's overriding interests are, of course, security and survival: to be a viable, prosperous and secure state living in peace with its neighbors and, in particular, with its contiguous neighbors: Syria, Lebanon, Jordan, Egypt and the Palestinians.

But, Israel is one of the few nations on earth that cannot describe to the rest of the world where its national borders lie. On that there is a wide divergence of opinion within the Israeli population. Opinions range from those who believe Israel is the land of the pre-1967 boundaries to those who, based on their religious views, believe God gave them "greater Israel"; that is, the entirety of the land from the Mediterranean east across the Jordan River. . . .

Former Israeli Prime Minister Menachim Begin, reflecting this latter view, once stated, "It would be impossible to annex the West Bank because it is already part of The Land." For the segment of the Israeli population who holds to the vision of a greater Israel, the country's interests do not seem to lie so much with peace, but in the fulfillment of what they truly believe is God's covenant promise to give all of 'the Land' to the Jews. While those who maintain this position are a minority, their position is intensely held.

Based on a myriad of opinion polls, it is clear, however, that a majority of Israelis not only want peace with their neighbors, but support a two-state solution and recognize that they will have to ultimately relinquish most, if not all, of the occupied territories.

The Way Forward: Begin at the End

Peace is only possible when both sides can begin to see the conflict through the eyes of their opponent. This obviously places a responsibility on both sides and it should go without saying that the Palestinians must make every effort to grasp the Israeli perspective. However, . . . I have opted to focus here almost exclusively on the Palestinian viewpoint, because it is so little understood in the United States.

Former Ambassador Philip Wilcox, President of the Foundation for Middle East Peace, captured the point well: "The Israeli-Palestinian struggle over the Holy Land . . . is the story of two victims. It is not surprising that neither the Jews, given their past suffering and desperation after Hitler's war, nor the Palestinians, who had no responsibility for Jewish suffering at the hands of Westerners, but nevertheless lost their homeland, felt any empathy for each other. It is tragic, nevertheless, that the passage of time has done so little to heal these historic wounds and that the rest of the world, especially the United States, has allowed this dreadful situation to fester."

So the struggle today is fundamentally over the land Israel conquered in 1967 and has settled since. Israel and the Palestinians—along with the U.S., the Europeans, Russia, the UN and other actors—have been trying—sporadically for a half century now to craft a fair and lasting peace. All to no avail.

The struggle today is fundamentally over the land Israel conquered in 1967 and has settled since.

Why? Primarily because previous American administrations have adopted a slow, gradualist approach that involved a series of small, incremental "confidence building" steps. This is the approach of the now famous—or infamous—"road map" that has been a road map to nowhere. The gradualist approach has not worked because there are important actors both in Israel and in the Palestinian community who do not want a negotiated settlement. And these actors have been able to sabotage or indefinitely delay (which is a form of sabotage) progress toward peace.

The Bush Administration's Efforts

[Since 2001], the Bush Administration has kept this whole problem simmering on 'low heat' on the back burner. Recently, Secretary of State [Condoleeza] Rice has been giving higher priority to resolving this conflict. She has called for the creation of a "political horizon" that describes the basic elements of an Israeli-Palestinian peace in a way that would restore hope and support for renewed negotiations. It would probably take much longer than the twenty-two months remaining [in Bush's term] for the Bush administration to negotiate a comprehensive peace. Yet if President Bush commits his administration to this goal and offers the kind of compelling "political horizon" that Condoleezza Rice has mentioned, but not yet defined, peace negotiations could overcome the current stalemate and at least pave the way to a final-status agreement.

Considering past failures of American peace efforts that did not define the endgame, the U.S. should avoid another drawn out, step-by-step process of confidence building and tentative accords on subsidiary issues. The 'road map' is a path to endless delay and obfuscation. The Palestinians, for their part, should not wait for a release of prisoners held by Israel or the elimination of Jewish settlements on the West Bank. Conversely, Israel should not wait for the Hamas-dominated Palestinian Authority to formally recognize Israel's right to exist or to forswear violence. These, on both sides, are rhetorical ploys and delaying tactics that serve only to keep the struggle grinding on.

Instead, Secretary Rice, with the President's full support, should move boldly and begin at the end by spelling out a "political horizon" at the end by offering clear American proposals for the issues of borders, sovereignty, the status of Jerusalem, the "right of return" for refugees, Israeli settlements in the West Bank, release of prisoners, and security guarantees. All of these issues must be negotiated, but the U.S. should offer its own vision of the answers, drawing on solutions that Israeli and Palestinians themselves have devised in official and unofficial negotiations over the last twenty years.

The United States, and only the United States, has the clout to move the parties forward along this path. Will it work? No one knows. But what we do know is that none of the gradualist approaches of the past have worked.

If Israel and the Palestinians cannot hammer out such an agreement, both will face an ongoing state of war with continued killing, destruction and economic hardship. And because this bleak scenario is also not in America's national interests, it is long past time that the Administration gives this noble effort its highest priority.

Continued U.S. Intervention in the Middle East Promotes Anti-Americanism and Terrorism

Leon Hadar

Leon Hadar is a Washington, D.C.–based journalist and author of the 2006 book Sandstorm: Policy Failure in the Middle East.

These days, conventional wisdom in Washington, DC holds that the Iraq War has been lost, that the Bush Doctrine of promoting unilateral regime change and spreading democracy in the Middle East has failed, and that the neoconservative ideologues who have dominated U.S. foreign policy since 9/11 are "out" while the realists are "in."

But the same conventional wisdom says you shouldn't hold your breath—even if an anti-war Democrat wins the White House in 2008, don't expect a revolutionary change in U.S. policy on the Middle East. In the best-case scenario, some U.S. troops would probably remain based in Iraq, and certainly in other parts of the Persian Gulf, as a way of demonstrating U.S. resolve to defend Saudi Arabia and the other oil-producing countries in the region; Washington would still maintain its strong military and economic support for Israel and try to mediate another peace process.

If anything, the election of one of the three leading . . . [Democratic] candidates, Sen. Hillary Clinton (D-NY), Sen. Barack Obama (D-NY), or former Sen. John Edwards (D-NC)—all of whom have little experience in national security—might make it more likely that the United States could be drawn into a military confrontation with Iran as the new

White House occupant tries to demonstrate that he or she is "tough." Hence, under either a Democratic or a Republican president, one should not be surprised to discover that the major element in the neoconservative agenda—maintaining U.S. military and diplomatic hegemony [dominance] in the Middle East—will likely remain alive and well, producing the never-ending vicious circle; more U.S. military interventions, leading to more anti-U.S. terrorism, resulting in more regime changes.

U.S. interventionism in the Middle East will [likely] continue ... [due to] the survival of ... [outdated U.S. policies based on] competition with the Soviet Union.

The Soviet Rationale

A lack of change in U.S. policy could be due to the power of inertia combined with the influences of the entrenched bureaucracies and powerful interest groups, the military-industrial complex, the "Israel Lobby," and the oil companies. But although all these players have major impacts on the policies pursued by the White House and Congress, the most important factor that makes it likely that U.S. interventionism in the Middle East will continue is the survival of what could be described as the U.S. Middle East Paradigm (MEP), whose origins go back to end of World War II and the start of the Cold War. Central to the MEP was the belief that competition with the Soviet Union made U.S. involvement in the Middle East a costly but necessary way to protect U.S. interests. The United States simply had to counter Soviet ambitions. Notwithstanding the end of the Cold War [the decades-long ideological struggle between the United States and the Soviet Union], the MEP has continued to dominate the thinking of policymakers, lawmakers, and pundits in Washington. To paraphrase the famous saying, policy paradigms don't die, and unlike old generals, they don't even fade away.

Three factors provided the rationale for ongoing U.S. involvement in the Middle East. The first was what were perceived as the necessities dictated by geo-strategy. The assumption was that the Soviet Union sought dominance in the region and had to be contained; consequently, the United States replaced Britain and France (which were militarily and economically weakened after World War II) in the role of protecting the interests of the Western alliance in the Middle East. The Soviet Union was an aggressive global power with a huge economic and military force and a crusading ideological disposition that was perceived to be as threatening to the West during the Cold War as Nazi Germany and Imperial Japan had been in World War II.

The second reason had to do with geo-economics. Given the larger context of the need to counter Soviet moves, Washington figured it was worth the price to be involved in the Middle East, not only to protect U.S. access to Mideast oil, but also to protect the free access of the Western economies to the energy resources in the Persian Gulf. It seemed to make strategic sense during the Cold War to let allies have a "free ride" on U.S. military power.

Third, with the establishment of Israel as a state in 1948, the United States underscored its historic and moral commitment [to] Israel's survival in the Middle East by helping it maintain its margin of security as it coped with hostile Arab neighbors. Throughout the Cold War, during which the Soviet Union worked to establish a beachhead in certain Arab states, this commitment evolved, at least in the minds of U.S. policymakers, from an essentially moral commitment into a geo-strategic one, with Israel seen as the one reliable democratic partner in the region.

These U.S. policies were very costly, involving alliances with military dictators and medieval despots and covert and overt military intervention. One example is when the United States helped depose a democratically elected government in

Iran and supported Saddam Hussein's confrontation with Iran. This policy ignited anti-Americanism in the Middle East. But if one accepted the notion that, based on calculations of national interest, Washington should have been engaged in the Middle East during the Cold War, one was also willing to accept the costs involved—including anti-Americanism that produced oil embargoes, embassies held hostage, and, of course, terrorism.

This essential paradigm has been accepted not only by U.S. neoconservatives, who have dominated post-9/11 U.S. foreign policy, but also by liberal internationalists and conservative and liberal realists. There may have been disagreements about tactics and emphasis among these elements of the U.S. foreign policy establishment, but all agreed that Washington should dominate policy in the region, or at least serve as balancer of last resort when conflicts arose.

The Effects of U.S. Mideast Policies

Even during the Cold War, this MEP led to contradictions that required delicate balancing by U.S. policymakers. Most of the oil-producing states, especially Saudi Arabia, seemed reliably anti-Soviet, but they were hardly pro-Israel, and from time to time they faced internal opposition that could upset their relationship with the United States and the West. So Washington had to appear to be always "doing something" to bring about an Israeli-Palestinian peace in order to keep the Arab oil-producing states on board.

At the same time, Washington seemed to see no alternative but to tolerate the extremely conservative, militant version of Islam, known as Wahhabism, which was dominant in Saudi Arabia. The Saud family considered it important, to maintain its power at home, not simply to tolerate Wahhabism, but also to promote and subsidize its spread overseas. [Al Qaeda terrorist leader] Osama bin Laden was a product of or at least heavily influenced by this branch of Islam. And both the

United States and Saudi Arabia believed it was in their interest to encourage and subsidize the essentially militant Islamic resistance to the Soviet occupation of Afghanistan during the 1980s. Hence, thousands of guerrilla fighters were trained in that conflict and, at least implicitly, encouraged to believe that once Soviet power in Afghanistan had been neutralized it was legitimate to look to a wider mission, which led eventually to blowback in the form of 9/11.

Within the Middle East, under the old MEP, Washington not only had to safeguard Israel, but also to placate Arab states by pressuring Israel to come to some kind of a negotiated peace settlement. Thus various U.S. administrations—[George H.W.] Bush and [Bill] Clinton—appllied pressure delicately on Israel to make concessions, all the while proclaiming their underlying loyalty to the idea of Israel as an independent Jewish state. This has proven to be a difficult job; despite Camp David meetings and the Oslo process, a peaceful resolution seems further away than ever. The Israelis and the Palestinians assume that Washington should reward them for making concessions that are perceived as "favors" for the Americans. At the same time, Arab and European governments reject responsibility for trying to help resolve the conflict.

U.S. Mideast Policies After the Cold War

During the Cold War, all these and other costs seemed to be justifiable because of the need to counter or neutralize Soviet influence. With the end of the Cold War, however, that factor receded in importance. But U.S. policymakers did not reassess the MEP for U.S. policy. Instead, during the administrations of Presidents George H.W. Bush and Bill Clinton, Washington took advantage of the Soviet collapse and the lack of competition from other global powers and emerged as the dominant power in the Middle East, including through the containment of Iraq and Iran, the extension of U.S. military power to the

Persian Gulf, and the efforts to mediate peace between Israel and Arab states. As a result of the emergence of a unipolar system with no checks-and-balances on U.S. power, the Middle East Paradigm survived and U.S. policy aimed to achieve strategic dominance in the Middle East.

U.S. policymakers need to recognize that the main rationale for U.S. intervention in the Middle East—the Soviet threat—has long since disappeared.

Indeed, from Gulf War I to Gulf War II there has been an effort to maintain that U.S. hegemony. Under Presidents Bush I and Clinton, this was done through a "cost-free" Pax Americana that included the dual containment of Iraq and Iran and creating the impression that Washington was trying to resolve the Palestinian-Israeli conflict. But this ignited more anti-Americanism and led to the second intifada [Pakistinian uprising] and perhaps 9/11, demonstrating that if you want hegemony, you pay for it. From this perspective, 9/11 should have been seen as a challenge to U.S. dominance in the Middle East. But again, no effort was made to reassess the MEP; in fact, the policy paradigm was the framework within which the U.S. response was fashioned. The neoconservatives simply offered a different strategy to achieve U.S. regional supremacy—through regime change and the direct occupation of Arab countries, instead of through the more diplomatic strategy and indirect military approach embraced by earlier administrations.

The costs of following neoconservatives' advice have become apparent. But most critics of the [George W.] Bush administration still fail to offer anything other than different strategies to achieve U.S. hegemony in the region; they prefer to maintain the current MEP instead of replacing the bankrupted policy paradigm by challenging the need for U.S. intervention in the Middle East.

Time for a New Policy

Indeed, U.S. policymakers need to recognize that the main rationale for U.S. intervention in the Middle East—the Soviet threat—has long since disappeared, and that U.S. military intervention in the region only ignites anti-Americanism in the form of international terrorism. Moreover, the U.S. economy is not dependent on Mideast oil; 70% of U.S. energy supplies do not originate in the Middle East. The United States is actually more dependent on Latin American oil than it is on Saudi and Persian Gulf oil. And the notion that U.S. policy in the Middle East helps give Americans access to cheap and affordable oil make little sense if one takes into consideration the military and other costs—including two Gulf Wars—that are added to the price that the U.S. consumer pays for driving his or her car.

With the demise of the Soviet threat, continued U.S. intervention in the [Mideast] region serves mainly to promote anti-Americanism and terrorism.

U.S. military force is quite likely not necessary to maintain access to Persian Gulf oil, either for the United States, Western Europe, or Japan. The oil-producing states have few resources other than oil, and if they don't sell it to somebody, they will have little wealth with which to maintain their power and curb domestic challenges. They need to sell oil more than the United States needs to buy it. If political and military influence is required to keep the oil flowing to Western Europe and Japan and increasingly to China, the countries that are truly dependent should be the ones to bear the cost.

The time has come, therefore, to bid farewell to the old MEP and try to draw the outlines of a new U.S. policy in the Middle East. There is a need for a long-term policy of U.S. "constructive disengagement" from the Middle East that will encourage the Europeans and other global and regional players to take upon themselves the responsibility of securing their interests in the region.

With the demise of the Soviet threat, continued U.S. intervention in the region serves mainly to promote anti-Americanism and terrorism. If a balancer of last resort is needed, let the European Union (EU), with its geographical proximity to and economic and demographic ties in the Middle East, do it. Likewise, the main threat to Israel's survival is not a lack of U.S. assistance, but Israel's control over the West Bank and Gaza and the continuing conflict with the Palestinians. U.S. support for Israel now creates disincentives for a settlement. The prospect of U.S. disengagement from the Middle East, and of a lower diplomatic profile in the Palestinian-Israeli dispute, should produce incentives for both sides, as well as for the Arab states and the EU, to deal with it.

Of course, the necessary condition for constructive disengagement from the Middle East is a larger U.S. reconsideration of the idea that Washington should be the final arbiter in disputes in the region and throughout the world, which would mean not only tolerating but also welcoming activity by the EU and other players. In that context, the foreign policy establishment in Washington would have to recognize that the Palestinian-Israeli conflict is now in the process of being "de-internationalized," transformed from a major regional conflict with enormous global ramifications for the United States and other global players, into a more "localized" affair that Washington, at the start of the 21st century, will be able to treat with a certain benign neglect.

Benign Neglect of the Middle East?

Detachment was certainly not the kind of frame of mind with which intellectual Washington's foreign policy elites and the U.S. public were conditioned to approach the Middle East for much of the Cold War. Hence, the notion of abandoning the MEP would certainly not be an easy process for U.S. policymakers and pundits. It's difficult to say goodbye to old friends. Just ask some of those veteran Cold Warriors in Washington. "Enemy deprivation syndrome" has been identified by psychiatrists as a common cause of anxiety among Washington's wonks [policy analysts].

Consequently, it is more likely that Washington will eventually pull back from its dominant role in the Middle East not through a responsible rethinking of U.S. engagement, but through a series of mounting costs and disasters that eventually lead to a "destructive disengagement" from the region that will look like—and to a great extent will be—a U.S. defeat and retreat. This is exactly what seems to be happening now.

But in case the next president does decide that the time has come to re-examine U.S. policy in the Middle East, here are a few pointers for a new Middle East Paradigm:

- Creating a new Congress of Vienna system—concert of Great Powers, a Northern Alliance that will include also the European Union (EU) and Russia, and eventually also China and India—will help contain instability and terrorism. The United States doesn't have the military power and economic resources to do that job alone. Washington needs to replace the concept of a U.S. Monopoly with that of a U.S.-led Global Oligopoly.

- In that context, Washington should encourage Europe to play a more activist role in the Middle East, which is, after all, its "strategic backyard." Besides the geographic proximity, Europe is also tied to the Middle East through demographic ties in the form of immigrants. European economies—not U.S. economies—are dependent on the energy resources in the Middle East. It's time for Washington to stop giving Europe a "free ride" in the Middle East and create incentives for them to start paying the costs of maintaining their geostrategic and geo-economic interests in the Middle East.

The deployment of the French and Italian peacekeeping troops in Lebanon is a step in the right direction.

- A new paradigm should shape incentives for the formation of regional balance of power systems that include Turkey, Israel, the leading Arab states, and Iran. Indeed, Washington needs to begin adjusting to the reality that Iran will become the hegemon [dominant power] in the Persian Gulf and that its nuclear military power will be counterbalanced by Israel.

- Adopt a policy of benign neglect toward the many tribal, ethnic, and religious conflicts in the Middle East. Washington needs to understand that it doesn't have the power to resolve or control all of them, and should engage in the Middle East through trade and investment and providing support to those who want to be allies. But by trying to force a U.S. mind-set and values on the nations of the Middle East, Washington will only erode its power and produce more anti-Americanism.

U.S. Military Actions in the Middle East Do Not Promote Security

Patrick Seale

Patrick Seale is a leading British writer on the Middle East, and the author of The Struggle for Syria *(1987);* Asad of Syria: The Struggle for the Middle East (1988); *and* Abu Nidal: A Gun for Hire *(1992).*

Afghanistan [was] on the agenda when NATO secretary general Jaap de Hoop Scheffer visit[ed] President George W. Bush at his Texas ranch on May 20–21 [2007]. The message de Hoop Scheffer ha[d] to convey [was] sombre: NATO [North Atlantic Treaty Organization] is losing the war against the Taliban. A fundamental policy review is urgently needed.

The most important new development is that the Afghans themselves, sickened by war and mounting civilian casualties, want the United States and other foreign troops to leave. As [Afghan] President Hamid Karzai himself admitted, Afghan patience with foreign troops is "wearing thin" five years after the U.S. invasion. "It is difficult for us to continue to tolerate civilian casualties," he said at a press conference [in May 2007].

On May 8, [2007,] the Senate in Kabul [the capital of Afghanistan] approved a bill that called for negotiations with the Taliban, a ceasefire, and a date for the withdrawal of foreign troops. The proposed legislation demands that foreign forces should not engage the Taliban unless they are themselves attacked or have first consulted with the Afghan army, police and government. The bill reflects a growing popular rebellion against heavy-handed American army tactics and aerial bombardments, which have brought death and destruction to many parts of Afghanistan. The bill has to be approved by the lower house of Parliament and by President Karzai before becoming law.

At much the same time in Baghdad, 144 members of Parliament—out of a total of 275—signed a petition calling for a timetable for the withdrawal of U.S. troops from Iraq. The petition is now being developed into a draft bill by the legal and foreign affairs committees of the Iraqi Parliament.

What seems clear is that the conflict in Afghanistan is widening and that pitched battles are taking place in many different parts of the country.

A Cause of Insecurity

Following talks with the Pakistan government . . . [in May 2007], de Hoop Scheffer himself declared that military force alone would not defeat the Taliban, but that reconstruction was the key to a durable peace in a country shattered by more than 25 years of conflict and civil war.

The problem, however, in both Afghanistan and Iraq is that, without security, no serious reconstruction can take place. The question arises, therefore, whether the violent campaigns against insurgents in both countries by U.S. and other foreign troops contribute to security or are themselves a cause of insecurity.

[In mid-May 2007,] the Taliban released a French aid worker captured more than a month [before]. Eric Damfreville arrived back in Paris on Saturday, exhausted by the harsh living-conditions, but saying that he had been well treated. He had been working in southwestern Afghanistan for Terre d'Enfrance, an agency that helps children. No one yet knows what deal the French may have struck with the Taliban behind the scenes to secure his release. A Taliban spokesman said Damfreville had been freed as a gesture to France's president

Nicolas Sarkozy. Perhaps more relevant was the statement Sarkozy made during his election campaign that there was no compelling reason for French troops to remain in Afghanistan.

Much like Prime Minister Nuri al-Maliki in Iraq, President Karzai's position in Afghanistan is increasingly uncomfortable. Crowds in the eastern city of Jalalabad have cried "Death to Karzai!" and "Death to Bush!" Violent anti-American demonstrations have taken place in Kabul, apparently sparked by the large-scale killing of civilians by American air strikes.

In the district of Shindand, 100 kilometres south of Herat, the U.S.-led coalition claimed to have killed 136 Taliban fighters at the end of [April 2007]. Local villagers said the dead were 51 civilians, among them 18 women and children. UN investigators said 1,600 families had been displaced. Another air strike on the village of Sarwan Qala destroyed several houses and is said to have killed between 50 and 80 civilians, mainly women and children. "Still now they are digging out bodies from the rubble," a local shopkeeper was quoted as saying.

What seems clear is that the conflict in Afghanistan is widening and that pitched battles are taking place in many different parts of the country, and not only in the east close to the Pakistan frontier and in the southern province of Helmand where the Taliban are well entrenched and where fierce fighting is continuing.

The correspondent of the *Financial Times* in Kabul reported on 4 May [2007] that [in April] the Taliban seized control of a highway just 70 kilometres from Kabul in the Tagab district of the central Kapisa province and held it for 24 hours, before being driven out by government forces. It was the heaviest battle in the region of the capital since 2001.

What [could] Jaap de Hoop Scheffer say to George W. Bush? His task [was] unenviable. The American president believes he is engaged in a 'global war on terror', but, in fact, the people his troops are fighting and killing are tribesmen seeking to defend their families and ancestral lands against foreigners. In Afghanistan, attachment to Islam and hatred of foreigners are both very great, and have defeated other armies, whether the Soviets in the 1980s or the British a century earlier.

The U.S. War in Iraq Is Pushing the Middle East Toward World War IV

Justin Raimondo

Justin Raimondo is an author and the editorial director of Anti-war.com, a Web site opposed to an interventionist U.S. foreign policy. He is also a contributing editor for the American Conservative, *a senior fellow at the Randolph Bourne Institute, and an adjunct scholar with the Ludwig von Mises Institute.*

As the situation on the ground in Iraq veers out of control, the rest of the Middle East is coming undone—a state of affairs directly attributable to our policy of "regime change" throughout the region.

On the western front, Lebanon is teetering on the brink of (yet another) civil war, with the very forces we have been backing covertly—al-Qaeda-affiliated Sunni radicals—in a stand-off with the (U.S.-allied) government of Prime Minister Fouad Siniora. With the Americans, the French, and assorted Euro-types standing behind them, the busybodies over at the UN—supposedly the world's major force for "peace"—have engineered a scenario whereby the Syrians and their Lebanese allies are being blamed for an assassination [of Lebanese prime minister Rafik Hariri] so mired in murk and mystery that it would take Sherlock Holmes on steroids to unravel it—and certainly the UN "investigation" has done nothing to solve this whodunit. The outcome is likely to be a UN-sponsored intervention that will be little more than a fig-leaf for American (and Israeli) meddling in the internal affairs of a supposedly sovereign nation—and, perhaps, a confrontation with Iran, which supports the nationalist-Shi'ite Hezbollah [a militant group].

Also on the western front: the Turks have launched what is to all intents and purposes an invasion of Kurdistan [a region in Iraq inhabited by the Kurds, a non-Arab people], sending thousands of troops into a region effectively controlled by the Kurdish Workers Party (PKK), a terrorist group that has wreaked death and destruction on thousands of Turkish civilians and foreign nationals over the years. The Turks legitimize this open violation of Iraqi sovereignty in the name of "hot pursuit," but of course they could pursue the terrorists all the way to Sulaimaniya, the regional capital, if they wanted to get at the true source of the PKK's support. They mounted this incursion in spite of strenuous warnings by the Americans that the consequences of such an act could be disastrous for US-Turkish relations—an indication of just how volatile this long-simmering issue has become.

The economic blowback from the outbreak of World War IV in the Middle East would strike a stunning blow to the American middle class.

To the east, Pakistan's crisis looms as potentially the biggest disaster of them all, one that would give a rather sinister meaning to the prospect of a Middle East meltdown—because Pakistan, after all, possesses nukes, the only Muslim nation so endowed. The result could well be a *nuclear* meltdown, with horrific consequences for the region and beyond. [Pakistani leader] General Pervez Musharraf's grip on power—never all that firm to begin with—is increasingly shaky, with the nation's Muslims in open rebellion, the National Assembly in an uproar over newly-imposed restrictions on the media, and much of the countryside slipping outside the General's control. If Muslim extremists succeed in toppling the Musharraf regime, the West could find itself confronted with a nuclearized ally of al-Qaeda ensconced in Islamabad.

Superimposed on the twin crises currently unfolding in Iraq and Iran—the former deteriorating into chaos and the latter just as rapidly rising to challenge American hegemony—these new threats to regional stability threaten to ignite a conflagration on a par with both world wars.

Economic Consequences for the United States

To begin with, the economic blowback from the outbreak of World War IV in the Middle East would strike a stunning blow to the American middle class—and, perhaps, drag us and much of the rest of the world into a downward spiral that would make the formerly "Great" Depression seem like a minor blip on the screen.

The economic costs of empire were calculated half a century ago by the Old Right seer [and journalist] Garet Garrett, who said part of the problem was that "everything goes out and nothing comes in." The American Imperium, Garrett averred, was an "empire of the Bottomless Purse"—and yet perhaps we will soon scrape bottom, having mortgaged our children, and *their* children, and exchanged our republic for what will surely go down in history as one of the biggest, and shortest-lived, empires of all time. An empire built on debt, an exercise in vanity and a monument to the hubris of our rulers: like the pyramids of Egypt, its relics will be the object of study and much wonder at how so great an effort could have been wasted on behalf of such a towering narcissism.

We have the mightiest military machine in human history, yet what do we have to show for it? In Iraq, we have an insurgency mounted by a rag-tag army of Ba'athist "dead-enders" and makeshift local militias that have fought us to a standstill. In the meantime, we have no effective defense against the day the Chinese and Japanese dump their dollars and stop subsidizing American militarism. No purse is bottomless: our empire of debt puts us at the mercy of our creditors.

The Threat of Terrorism

America's imperial aspirations are also cause to fear a threat on yet another front: as 9/11 proved, "blowback" is likely to hit us on our own soil. It behooves us to remember that, for all the diversions away from our real enemies, al-Qaeda and its satellites around the globe, we do indeed face the very real threat of a 9/11-like attack in the continental US. This, after all, has always been the linchpin of Osama bin Laden's strategic line: that, rather than conducting guerrilla operations around the edges of the empire—say, against Israel, or the local U.S.-supported tyrants, such as Hosni Mubarak [the president of Egypt] and the House of Saud [the ruling family of Saudi Arabia]—it is necessary to hit the Americans where they live.

> *We are hurtling toward catastrophe in the Middle East at such speeds that it seems almost impossible to slow down . . . the momentum for war.*

Seismic tremors—rippling outward from the center of the earthquake set off by the invasion and ongoing war in Iraq—are shaking the entire region, and the shockwaves are sure to hit Washington, London, Paris, and Tokyo with gale force. Whether our fragile freedoms and the bubble of inflated prosperity will survive the storm is an open question, but of one thing we can be sure: we're about to be tested as never before.

Will the United States Survive?

Given the sorry record of the past five years or so, I'm not at all confident that we'll muddle through, this time, without losing a lot of what America—and the developed world, often known as "the West"—used to be about. It's at times like these that I wish I was religious, in the true sense of the word, and could put my faith in Providence as the ultimate guarantor of

American liberty and our republican traditions, but, unfortunately, I find that impossible. Although I am not evangelical in my atheistic fervor, and give moral credence to religiously-motivated resistance to militarism and authoritarianism, the only sort of faith I can claim is full confidence in the power of ideas. Specifically the power of the libertarian and anti-imperialist ideas that generated the American Revolution—and hold out the promise of sparking yet another.

My great fear, however, is that it is too late for that. We are hurtling toward catastrophe in the Middle East at such speeds that it seems almost impossible to slow down, let alone reverse, the momentum for war. With lemming-like determination, our rulers seem intent on leaping over the Middle East precipice and into an abyss. Who will stand in the path of the War Party as it force-marches a reluctant nation into battle, this time against the entire Muslim world? Like that lone Chinese dissident who stood in the pathway of a Red Army tank during the Tiananmen Square protests, such a leader would have to possess the kind of courage that surpasses all reason—and where are such people to be found?

Surely not on the stage of either party's presidential debates, unless we're talking about Ron Paul or the Democrats' Cassandra, Mike Gravel. Gravel is not a real factor, except as a provocateur to show up the cowardice and opportunism of the "majors." However, Ron Paul is a different matter: his candidacy could easily set off the sort of ideological avalanche that paleoconservatives and many libertarians have long awaited, one that could eventually sweep away the neoconservative hegemony over the GOP [Republican Party] and help return the Republicans to their anti-interventionist, pro-individual rights roots. This, however, is a long-term project, one that cannot be achieved in the course of a single election season, and that's the problem: we don't have a lot of time.

The spark was struck when we invaded and occupied Iraq, and the fuse is now burned nearly to the end. If our republic survives the inevitable explosion, it will be in some permanently disfigured form—an America rendered unrecognizable not only to the shades of the Founders, but to ourselves.

Organizations to Contact

The editors have compiled the following list of organizations concerned with the issues debated in this book. The descriptions are derived from materials provided by the organizations. All have publications or information available for interested readers. The list was compiled on the date of publication of the present volume; names, addresses, phone and fax numbers, and e-mail and Web site addresses may change. Be aware that many organizations take several weeks or longer to respond to inquiries, so allow as much time as possible.

American-Israeli Cooperative Enterprise (AICE)
2810 Blaine Dr., Chevy Chase, MD   20815
(301) 565-3918 • fax: (301) 587-9056
e-mail: mgbard@aol.com
Web site: www.us-israel.org

AICE is a nonprofit, nonpartisan organization that seeks to strengthen the U.S.-Israel relationship by developing social and educational programs that emphasize common values. AICE also works to enhance Israel's image by publicizing Israeli solutions to these problems. Its Web site includes numerous reports as well as the Jewish Virtual Library, a comprehensive online encyclopedia of Jewish history.

American Jewish Committee (AJC)
PO Box 705, New York, NY   10150
(212) 715-4000 • fax: (212) 891-1450
e-mail: pr@ajc.org
Web site: www.ajc.org

AJC is an international think tank and pro-Israel advocacy organization that works to strengthen U.S.-Israel relations, build international support for Israel, and support the Israeli-Arab peace process. AJC's Web site contains links to breaking news stories, opinion surveys, and a wealth of AJC articles and publications, including, the reports *Israel's Quest for Peace* and *Syria: Brokering Hate on Israel's Border.*

Americans for Middle East Understanding (AMEU)
475 Riverside Dr., Room 245, New York, NY 10115-0245
(212) 870-2053 • fax: (212) 870-2050
e-mail: info@ameu.org
Web site: www.ameu.org

AMEU is an organization founded to foster a better understanding in America of the history, goals, and values of Middle Eastern cultures and peoples, the rights of Palestinians, and the forces shaping U.S. policy in the Middle East. AMEU publishes the *Link*, a bimonthly newsletter, as well as books and pamphlets on the Middle East.

Arab American Institute (AAI)
1600 K St. NW, Suite 601, Washington, DC 20006
(202) 429-9210 • fax: (202) 429-9214
e-mail: jzogby@aaiusa.org
Web site: www.aaiusa.org

The AAI represents the interests of Arab Americans in the United States and serves as a resource for government officials, the media, political leaders, and others on public policy issues that concern Arab Americans and U.S-Arab relations. The AAI Web site contains numerous links to articles about the Middle East and its conflicts.

Foundation for Middle East Peace
1763 N St. NW, Washington, DC 20036
(202) 835-3650 • fax: (202) 835-3651
e-mail: info@fmep.org
Web site: www.fmep.org

The Foundation for Middle East Peace is a nonprofit organization that promotes a peaceful resolution of the Israeli-Palestinian conflict. To do this, it sponsors programs and public speaking, makes small financial grants, and publishes the bimonthly *Report on Israeli Settlements in the Occupied Territories*, which contains analysis and commentary on the Arab-Israeli conflict.

Institute for Palestine Studies (IPS)

3501 M St. NW, Washington, DC   20007
(202) 342-3990 • fax: (202) 342-3927
e-mail: ipsbrt@palestine-studies.org
Web site: www.palestine-studies.org

IPS is a private nonprofit, pro-Arab institute unaffiliated with any political organization or government. Established in 1963 in Beirut, the institute promotes research, analysis, and documentation of the Arab-Israeli conflict and its resolution. IPS publishes quarterlies in three languages and maintains offices all over the world. The institute's U.S. branch publishes four quarterly journals in three languages, including the *Journal of Palestinian Studies* and the *Jerusalem Quarterly*, as well as numerous books and articles on the Arab-Israeli conflict and Palestinian affairs.

Middle East Forum

1500 Walnut St., Suite 1050, Philadelphia, PA   19102
(215) 546-5406 • fax: (215) 546-5409
e-mail: info@meforum.org
Web site: www.meforum.org

The Middle East Forum is a think tank that works to define and promote American interests in the Middle East. It supports strong American ties with Israel, Turkey, and other democracies as they emerge. It publishes the *Middle East Quarterly*, a policy-oriented journal, and its Web site includes articles, summaries of activities, and a discussion forum.

Middle East Institute

1761 N St. NW, Washington, DC   20036-2882
(202) 785-1141 • fax: (202) 331-8861
e-mail: mideasti@mideasti.org

Web site: www.themiddleeastinstitute.org

The Middle East Institute's mission is to promote better understanding of Middle Eastern cultures, languages, religions, and politics. It publishes numerous books, papers, audiotapes, and videos as well as the quarterly *Middle East Journal.*

Middle East Media Research Institute (MEMRI)
PO Box 27837, Washington, DC   20038-7837
(202) 955-9070 • fax: (202) 955-9077
e-mail: memri@memri.org
Web site: www.memri.org

MEMRI is a nonprofit, nonpartisan organization that translates and disseminates articles and commentaries from Middle East media sources and provides analysis on the political, ideological, intellectual, social, cultural, and religious trends in the region.

Middle East Network Information Center (MENIC)
University of Texas, Austin, TX   78712
(512) 471-3881 • fax: (512) 471-7834
e-mail: cmes@menic.texas.edu
Web site: http://menic.utexas.edu

MENIC is an online guide to Middle East–related Web sites and databases that can be accessed via the World Wide Web. It is created by a staff of editors who visit and evaluate Web sites and then organize them into subject-based categories and sub-categories.

Middle East Policy Council (MEPC)
1730 M St. NW, Suite 512, Washington, DC   20036-4505
(202) 296-6767 • fax: (202) 296-5791
e-mail: info@mepc.org
Web site: www.mepc.org

MEPC is a nonprofit educational organization founded in 1981 to promote a full discussion of issues affecting U.S. policy in the Middle East for U.S. policy makers. It publishes the quarterly journal *Middle East Policy.*

Middle East Research and Information Project (MERIP)

1500 Massachusetts Ave. NW, Washington, DC   20005
(202) 223-3677 • fax: (202) 223-3604
Web site: www.merip.org

MERIP is a nonprofit, nongovernmental organization established to provide information and analysis on the Middle East to the media. It seeks to educate the public about the contemporary Middle East with particular emphasis on U.S. foreign policy, human rights, and social-justice issues. It publishes the bimonthly *Middle East Report.*

United States Department of State, Bureau of Near Eastern Affairs

2201 C St. NW, Washington, DC   20520
(202) 647-4000
Web site: www.state.gov/p/nea/

The Bureau of Near Eastern Affairs deals with U.S. foreign policy and U.S. relations with the countries in the Middle East and North Africa. Its Web site offers country information as well as news briefings and press statements on U.S. foreign policy.

Washington Institute for Near East Policy

1828 L St. NW, Suite 1050, Washington, DC   20036
(202) 452-0650 • fax: (202) 223-5364
e-mail: info@washingtoninstitute.org
Web site: www.washingtoninstitute.org

The institute is an independent, nonprofit research organization that provides information and analysis on the Middle East and U.S. policy in the region. It publishes numerous books, periodic monographs, and reports on regional politics, security, and economics, including *PolicyWatch/PeaceWatch,* which focuses on the Arab-Israeli peace process.

Web Sites

BBC News: Middle East
(http://news.bbc.co.uk/2/hi/middle_east/default.stm)

This Web site is run by the British Broadcasting Company and provides up-to-date news on Middle East events.

Bitterlemons.org
(www.bitterlemons.org)

This Web site presents Israeli and Palestinian viewpoints on the Palestinian-Israeli conflict and peace process as well as related regional issues of concern.

Global Connections
(www.pbs.org/wgbh/globalconnections/mideast/index.html)

A Web site operated by public television that provides time-lines and background information about Middle East geography, religion, culture, science, and politics.

Haaretz.com
(www.haaretz.com/)

This is an online edition of one of the leading Israeli newspapers published in English.

Islamic Republic News Agency
(www2.irna.com/en/)

This agency of the government of Iran provides links to news articles and current affairs about that nation and the Middle East.

The Israeli-Palestinian Conflict
(www.washingtonpost.com/wp-dyn/world/issues/mideast peace/)

A *Washington Post* special report on the Israeli-Palestinian conflict in the Middle East.

Mideast: Land of Conflict
(www.cnn.com/SPECIALS/2003/mideast/)

A CNN site that provides useful background information on the Arab-Israeli conflict.

MidEastWeb
(www.mideastweb.org/)

MidEastWeb is a site founded by people from different nations who are active in peace education efforts. It features articles and opinions about events in the region as well as maps and a history of the conflict in the Middle East.

Bibliography

Books

Jeremy Bowen
Six Days: How the 1967 War Shaped the Middle East. New York: Thomas Dunne, 2005.

Rachel Bronson
Thicker than Oil: America's Uneasy Partnership with Saudi Arabia. New York: Oxford University Press, 2006.

Jimmy Carter
Palestine: Peace, Not Apartheid. New York: Simon & Schuster, 2006.

Christopher Catherwood
A Brief History of the Middle East. New York: Carroll & Graf, 2006.

David Downing
The Making of the Middle East. Chicago: Raintree, 2006.

Galia Golan
Israel and Palestine: Peace Plans and Proposals from Oslo to Disengagement. Princeton, NJ: Markus Wiener, 2006.

Dilip Hiro
War Without End: The Rise of Islamist Terrorism and the Global Response. New York: Routledge, 2002.

Antonia Juhasz
The Bush Agenda: Invading the World, One Economy at a Time. New York: Reagan, 2006.

John King
Oil in the Middle East. Chicago: Raintree, 2006.

Michael T. Klare	*Blood and Oil: The Dangers and Consequences of America's Growing Dependency on Imported Petroleum*. New York: Metropolitan, 2004.
Bernard Lewis	*The Crisis of Islam: Holy War and Unholy Terror*. New York: Modern Library, 2003.
Seyyed Vali Reza Nasr	*The Shia Revival: How Conflicts Within Islam Will Shape the Future*. New York: Norton, 2006.
Michael B. Oren	*Power, Faith, and Fantasy: America in the Middle East, 1776 to the Present*. New York: Norton, 2007.
Dan Smith	*The State of the Middle East: An Atlas of Conflict and Resolution*. Berkeley and Los Angeles: University of California Press, 2006.
Shibley Telhami	*The Stakes: America and the Middle East*. Denver, CO: Westview, 2002.
Sandy Tolan	*The Lemon Tree: An Arab, a Jew, and the Heart of the Middle East*. New York: Bloomsbury, 2006.
Milton Viorst	*Storm from the East: The Struggle Between the Arab World and the Christian West*. New York: Modern Library, 2006.

Periodicals

Christopher Allbritton and Phil Zabriskie
"Families Held Captive," *Time International*, July 17, 2006.

America
"Beyond the Blame Game," May 21, 2007.

Ramzy Baroud
"Middle East Peace Process: Stagnation by Design," *Global Research*, December 23, 2006. www.globalresearch.ca/index.php?context=viewArticle&code=20061223&articleId=4254.

John Gee
"Looming Energy Crunch Fuels International Conflict and Instability," *Washington Report on Middle East Affairs*, July 2005.

Stephen Glain
"Mullahs Gone Mild; Don't Look Now, but the Face of Radical Islam Has Changed Dramatically Across the Middle East," *Newsweek International*, April 30, 2007.

Global Agenda
"A Chronology of the Middle East Conflict," February 9, 2005.

Steve Hargreaves
"And Iraq's Big Oil Contracts Go to . . . Companies from China, India and Other Asian Nations Are Seen Getting the First Contracts. But Don't Write Off Big Oil Just Yet," *CNNmoney.com*, April 5 2007. http://money.cnn.com/2OO7/O4/O5/news/international/iraq_oil/index.htm.

Andrew I. Killgore	"Burning Issues: Understanding and Misunderstanding the Middle East: A 40-Year Chronicle," *Washington Report on Middle East Affairs*, July 2007.
Michael Lerner	"When Will They Ever Learn? How to Overcome the Middle East Mess," *Tikkun*, September/October 2006.
Edward Luttwak	"The Middle of Nowhere," *Prospect*, April 27, 2007. www.prospect-maga zine.co.uk/ article_details.php?id=9302.
Scott MacLeod	"Why Lebanon Is Erupting Again," *Time International*, June 4, 2007.
Robert W. McElroy	"Why We Must Withdraw from Iraq: An Argument from Catholic Just-War Principles," *America*, April 30, 2007.
Bobby Muller	"A Broken Contract: Returning Service Members Deserve Better," *America*, May 28, 2007.
Edmund O'Sullivan	"Irish Formula Could Win the Global War Against Terrorism: It Is a Long Way from Ireland to the Front Line of America's Global War on Terror. But Lessons from Ulster Could Form the Foundations of a Road Map to Peace in the Middle East," *Middle East Economic Digest*, May 18, 2007.

Jane Bryant
Quinn
"The Price of Our Addiction; For Years to Come, We'll Be Paying for Our Oil in Both Treasure and Blood, as We Fight and Parley to Keep Ever-Tighter Supplies Flowing Our Way," *Newsweek*, April 24, 2006.

Khaled Abu
Toameh
"A Ghastly Little Place: The Fate of the Gaza Strip," *National Review*, June 25, 2007.

*Washington
Report on Middle
East Affairs*
"Water: Fuel for Conflict in the Middle East," July/August 2003.

Kevin Whitelaw
"A Resurgent Menace," *U.S. News & World Report*, May 14, 2007.

Ann Wright
"What Congress Really Approved: Benchmark No. 1: Privatizing Iraq's Oil for US Companies," *Z Magazine*, May 26, 2007. www.zmag.org/content/showarticle.cfm?ItemID=12919.

Fareed Zakaria
"Islam and Power; Is President Bush's Plan to Spread Democracy Turning into a Fiasco? It Doesn't Have To. But It Does Need to Change," *Newsweek*, February 13, 2006.

Index